P9-EGD-623

superlegumes

eat your way to great health

CHRISSY FREER

superlegumes

eat your way to great health

CHRISSY FREER

pp t t

by RANDOM HOUSE

Abington Free Library
1030 Old York Road
Abington, PA 19001-4534

FEB 15 2016

contents

introduction

When we think of legumes, we typically think of the legumes we eat as dried seeds — white beans, chickpeas, borlotti beans, adzuki beans, kidney beans, pinto beans, dried peas, black beans, lentils, and the like. All are delicious, versatile, and nutritious. But we tend not to think of the legumes that are eaten fresh, such as green peas, crisp soy beans, crunchy green beans, brightly colored borlotti beans, and young fava beans. The legume family also encompasses such surprising members as carob, mesquite, lupins, and even peanuts. This book explores legumes in all their many and varied states.

What all legumes have in common is that they're members of the Fabaceae family. It's an extensive family, comprising some 13,000 different species grown worldwide. All legumes produce seed-bearing pods, and when the seeds are dried, they're sometimes referred to as pulses.

Legumes are whole foods — that is, foods as close to their natural state as possible. The health and nutritional benefits of eating a diet rich in whole foods is starting to gain the recognition it deserves, especially in light of the abundance of highly processed foods that line the shelves of our supermarkets.

"Whole food" doesn't need to mean food that is time consuming or fiddly to prepare. Legumes are readily available, easy to cook, inexpensive compared to other protein sources, suitable for a wide range of cooking styles, and very flavorful.

What's more, legumes are nutritional powerhouses, among nature's true "super foods." Eating legumes regularly has been linked to numerous health and nutritional benefits.

Nutritional benefits of legumes

Legumes are not only high in carbohydrates, fiber, and protein, they're also rich in several micronutrients including B-group vitamins, iron, calcium, phosphorus, zinc, and magnesium. Legumes are a good source of folate (essential for women of child-bearing age) and antioxidants. They're low in saturated fats, they're gluten-free, and they have a low glycemic index (GI).

Protein Protein plays an important role throughout the human body; it is essential for growth and repair.

Legumes are an extremely valuable protein source, particularly for vegetarians and vegans, and they typically comprise 25–30% protein. Three-quarters of a cup to one cup (4–5 oz) of cooked legumes is considered a serving of protein, and it is recommended that we eat two to three servings of protein per day.

Proteins are made up of building blocks called amino acids, which can be classified as essential or non-essential. Essential amino acids must be consumed in the diet because they can't be made by the body; there are nine of these. If a protein contains all nine essential amino acids, it is referred to as a complete protein.

Soy beans are a particularly notable source of protein because they contain all the essential amino acids, which makes them a complete protein.

However, even legumes that don't contain all the essential amino acids form a complete protein when combined with a whole grain, such as rice or corn. Legumes have traditionally been served with grains in many cultures – think of staple combinations such as lentils and rice, or black beans and grits.

It's not necessary, though, to consume all the components of a complete protein in one sitting to gain its benefits. A diet of nutritious foods – including legumes and whole grains – eaten over the course of a day will provide all the essential amino acids.

Fiber There are two main types of dietary fiber: soluble and insoluble. Legumes are rich in both.

Soluble fiber attracts water and forms a thick gel-like substance during digestion, in turn slowing down the digestive process. This can slow the absorption of sugar, resulting in lower blood sugar levels. Soluble fiber can also assist in heart health by lowering "bad" blood cholesterol.

Insoluble fiber, in contrast, doesn't dissolve in water. It passes through the digestive tract intact, adding bulk to stools and therefore helping food pass through more quickly. This can assist in preventing constipation and irritable bowel, as well as keeping the colon healthy. A diet high in insoluble fiber has been linked to a reduced risk of some cancers, especially colon cancer.

Weight control The relationship between legumes and weight management is multifaceted. As already mentioned, their high fiber content helps to provide an early sensation of fullness and can help trigger the feeling of having had enough to eat. This can result in lower overall food consumption and lower energy intake.

The low GI value of legumes acts to slow the absorption of glucose into the bloodstream, resulting in greater insulin sensitivity and improved secretion of hormones such as leptin, which helps regulate the amount of fat stored in the body.

Diets high in protein have been linked to weight control and even weight loss, and legumes are high-protein foods. What's more, you can eat a generous serving of legumes without consuming a lot of fat or calories.

All these factors make legumes an invaluable aid in long-term weight control.

Glycemic index and diabetes management
The glycemic index (GI) ranks foods according to the effect of their carbohydrates on blood glucose levels. Low-GI foods release glucose slowly, resulting in steady, sustained energy levels. In contrast, high-GI foods release glucose quickly and cause sudden spikes in blood sugar. A low-GI diet is essential in the management of diabetes. Legumes are among the lowest GI foods, which makes them ideal for people with diabetes.

Fighting cancer and disease
Legumes contain various phytochemicals (such as anti-oxidants, flavonoids, and isoflavones) that have been linked to a reduced risk of certain cancers and diseases such as heart disease. Soy beans, in particular, are among the richest sources of isoflavones, which have been linked to various health benefits, including easing of menopausal symptoms in women, reduced risk of osteoporosis, and reduced risk of certain cancers such as breast cancer.

Digestive issues
Eating a lot of legumes (particularly dried ones) can cause digestive discomfort for some people – abdominal bloating and gas are not uncommon. The source of the problem is the carbohydrate sugars (oligosaccharides) that legumes contain.
But there are some things you can do to minimize or eliminate the effects:
- Always soak dried legumes (other than lentils) before cooking them. Even better, change the soaking water once or twice.
- After soaking, rinse the legumes again before cooking them.
- Rinse canned legumes thoroughly before using.
- If you're not used to eating legumes, introduce them into your diet gradually, so your body can adjust. The symptoms tend to decrease over time.

Increasing legumes in your diet
Legumes are unique in belonging to not one but two of the main food groups in the dietary guidelines: vegetables and proteins. Most of us don't eat a lot of legumes, yet they're so easy to incorporate into meals. Here are some simple ways to add legumes to your diet:
- Try adding half a cup of cooked red kidney beans, black beans, or white beans to your breakfast omelet or scrambled eggs.
- Canned legumes such as chickpeas, lentils, white beans, or kidney beans make a super-fast and nutritious addition to your lunchtime salad. Simply combine them with some mixed salad leaves, cherry tomatoes, cucumber, and avocado. For an extra protein hit, add a can of tuna or some cooked chicken.
- Add half a cup of beans to your lunchtime wrap, or spread your sandwich, crackers, or bread roll with hummus or white bean dip instead of fat-laden mayonnaise.

- Replace your regular mashed potatoes with a white bean or chickpea mash. For a creamy white bean mash without all the fat, stir in a little ricotta before serving.
- Legumes can be added to your favorite stews, casseroles, pasta sauces (such as bolognese), and curries to replace some or all of the meat. Not only does this increase the overall nutritional value of the meal – adding a good dose of dietary fiber, vitamins, minerals, and protein – it also reduces the cost.
- When cooking rice, toss in a handful of brown or green lentils as well.
- Next time you're making muffins, cookies, cakes, or even desserts, replace some of the fat and flour with mashed beans. This reduces the overall fat and calorie content, and adds good amounts of protein and fiber.

Dried versus canned legumes

Either dried or canned legumes can be used in almost all the recipes in this book. Dried ones are more economical and contain no additives (such as salt), but it's invaluable to keep a supply of canned ones in the cupboard too because they're so convenient. Nutritionally speaking, there's virtually no difference between dried and canned legumes.

When you're shopping for the canned version, read the labels and choose products with no or little added salt – the salt content varies a lot from one brand to the next.

And here's a handy tip for cooking dried legumes: cook more than you need, then divide the extras among small resealable bags, including a little of the cooking liquid. Seal and freeze. Then you'll always have cooked legumes on hand to add to your soups and casseroles.

Environmental benefits

As well as being good to eat, legumes are an environmentally friendly, sustainable source of dietary protein.

Think of the amount of plant food it takes to feed a cow in order to produce a pound of beef, and the amount of land needed to grow that plant food. Compare that with eating high-protein plant foods (such as legumes) instead. Sheep and cattle have a conversion efficiency rate of feed to bodyweight of only around 15%, pigs around 30%, and poultry around 50%. This efficiency is further reduced when converted to yield of edible protein.

Legumes, more than many other plants, have other environmental benefits too. When they grow, legumes develop root nodules containing special bacteria that convert atmospheric nitrogen into ammonia, which in turn is used by the plant to produce plant protein. When the plant dies, residual plant nitrogen is returned to the soil for use by the next crop. For this very reason, legumes are often grown in rotation with other crops that can't fix atmospheric nitrogen. Legumes, and the crops that follow, can be grown without the costly synthetic nitrogenous fertilizers that can increase soil acidity and pollute waterways.

Other differences in the environmental effects of meat production compared to legume production include their contributions to greenhouse gas emissions. Sheep and cattle produce and emit significant amounts of methane into the atmosphere as a by-product of their digestive process. Plants (including legumes), in contrast, remove carbon dioxide from the atmosphere during their growth cycle via photosynthesis.

Cooking guide

SEVERAL FACTORS AFFECT the cooking time required for legumes. These include the age of the legumes (the older they are, the longer they take to cook), the presoaking time, the storage conditions, and even the humidity. Therefore the cooking times indicated in this chart are intended only as a guide. The legumes in your pantry might take more or less time to cook.

When legumes are sufficiently cooked, they should look plump and tender. Their skins may start to split a little (especially in the case of chickpeas), but they should be mainly intact.

Legumes generally swell during cooking to about one-and-a-half times their dried size. They should retain their shape – the aim in most cases is not to

Legume	1 cup dried	Yield, cooked and drained	Soaking time	Cooking time – stovetop, presoaked	Cooking time – pressure cooker, presoaked	Cooking time – pressure cooker, not presoaked
Adzuki beans	6⅞ oz	3 cups	Overnight	30–45 minutes	5–10 minutes	15–20 minutes
Black beans	7¾ oz	2¾ cups	Overnight	45 minutes–1 hour	5–10 minutes	10–20 minutes
Borlotti beans	6¾ oz	2½ cups	Overnight	45 minutes–1 hour	10–15 minutes	30–35 minutes
Cannellini beans	6⅞ oz	3 cups	Overnight	45 minutes–1 hour	5–10 minutes	20–25 minutes
Chickpeas (garbanzo beans)	7 oz	2⅔ cups	Overnight	45 minutes–1 hour	15–20 minutes	30–40 minutes
Fava beans (broad beans)	6¾ oz	2½ cups	Overnight	45 minutes–1 hour	10–15 minutes	25–30 minutes
Kidney beans	6¾ oz	2¾ cups	Overnight	45 minutes–1 hour	10–15 minutes	20–25 minutes

cook them into mush, although exceptions may include red lentils and split peas, depending on the recipe. They should have a creamy, fluffy texture, and be a consistent color throughout (a darker spot in the middle indicates they are not cooked all the way through). Their flavor should be nutty, even slightly meaty, with no "raw" taste.

Pressure cookers offer a quick way to cook legumes. Note, however, that the manufacturers of some pressure cookers recommend against cooking certain legumes by this method because they tend to foam and clog the valve. This applies particularly to split peas and split lentils, such as red lentils. Check your pressure cooker's instruction manual.

Legume	1 cup dried	Yield, cooked and drained	Soaking time	Cooking time – stovetop, presoaked	Cooking time – pressure cooker, presoaked	Cooking time – pressure cooker, not presoaked
Lentils – brown or green	$7^2/_3$ oz	3 cups	Not necessary	20–25 minutes	8–10 minutes	8–10 minutes
Lentils – Puy	$7^1/_2$ oz	3 cups	Not necessary	25–30 minutes	10–12 minutes	10–12 minutes
Lima beans (butter beans)	$6^3/_4$ oz	$2^1/_2$ cups	Overnight	45 minutes–1 hour	5–10 minutes	12–15 minutes
Navy beans (haricot beans)	$7^3/_4$ oz	$2^2/_3$ cups	Overnight	1–$1^1/_2$ hours	10–15 minutes	20–30 minutes
Pinto beans	7 oz	$2^2/_3$ cups	Overnight	1 hour	10–15 minutes	20–30 minutes
Soy beans	$6^1/_2$ oz	$2^2/_3$ cups	Overnight	1–$1^1/_2$ hours	10–15 minutes	25–35 minutes
Split peas – green or yellow	$7^3/_4$ oz	$2^2/_3$ cups	Overnight (optional)	30–45 minutes	5–10 minutes	5–10 minutes

chickpeas

chickpeas

CHICKPEAS, ALSO KNOWN as garbanzo beans, are one of the earliest cultivated legumes, dating back some 7500 years to the Middle East. The plant is small with feathery leaves, and it bears seedpods containing two or three peas per pod.

There are two main varieties of chickpeas, distinguished by their seed size, shape, color, and end use.

Desi chickpeas, the smaller variety, are angular and wrinkled in appearance, and they range in color from brown to fawn, yellow, orange, black, or green. They are normally sold hulled and split, or ground into flour.

Kabuli chickpeas are larger and rounder than desi chickpeas. The canned and dried chickpeas available from supermarkets are most often kabuli chickpeas. White to cream in color, they are known for their nutty flavor. They are generally used whole and are typically found in Middle Eastern and Mediterranean dishes. Kabuli chickpeas have a higher starch content than the desi variety, and less fiber.

Less common varieties include Bombay, or Bambai, chickpeas, which are similar in color to the desi variety but slightly larger. These are popular in the Indian subcontinent. Ceci neri are larger and darker than desi peas, and are grown only in Italy.

Chickpea flour, also known as besan or gram flour, is widely used throughout India to make pancakes, crepes, flat breads, batters, and fritters. Besan flour is naturally gluten-free, and it can be used in combination with other gluten-free flours in baked goods. Look for chickpea flour in supermarkets, health food stores, and Indian grocery stores.

Chickpeas have a delicious nutty taste and are extremely versatile in the kitchen. They make a delicious, filling, and healthy addition to salads, soups, stews, and casseroles. They can be roasted to produce a crunchy snack, or "popped" in a heated pan with a little oil as an alternative to traditional popcorn. Fresh green chickpeas can also be eaten as a green vegetable, the peas picked out of the pod and eaten raw and the leaves used in salads.

The nutty, buttery flavor of chickpeas combines well with dried spices, garlic, and herbs. Chickpeas are the key ingredient in such classic dishes as the Indian curry chana masala, and the Middle Eastern falafel and hummus (the Arabic translation of "chickpeas" is "hummus").

Chickpeas are an excellent source of low-fat plant protein. They're also gluten-free and low GI, providing slow-release energy. This is particularly important for people with diabetes, but everyone can benefit from it.

Their high level of soluble fiber can assist with weight management by leaving you feeling full for longer, which means you eat less overall. In addition, their high level of insoluble fiber (fiber that passes through the system undigested) assists heart health and helps to prevent constipation and irritable bowel, keeping your colon healthy.

Another impressive quality of chickpeas is their rich antioxidant and phytonutrient content, which is found mainly in their outer layer. Antioxidants and phytonutrients play an essential role in the body, helping eliminate free radicals, reducing the risk of certain diseases, having anti-inflammatory effects, and helping support our lungs and cardiovascular and nervous systems.

Chickpeas are a valuable source of folate, manganese, copper, iron, and phosphorus.

NUTRITION	PER 100 G (3½ OZ) COOKED CHICKPEAS
Energy	111 cal
Protein	6.3 g
Fat	2.1 g
Saturated fat	0.2 g
Carbohydrate	13.3 g
Dietary fiber	4.7 g
Folate	63 µg
Iron	1.8 mg
Phosphorus	86 mg

Cooking instructions

Stovetop

Soak 1 cup dried chickpeas in cold water overnight. Rinse well, then drain. Put them in a large saucepan, add water to cover the chickpeas by 2 inches, and bring to the boil. Reduce the heat to low and simmer for 45 minutes–1 hour or until tender. Drain.

If using unsoaked chickpeas, cook for an extra 30–45 minutes.

Pressure cooker

Soak 1 cup dried chickpeas in cold water overnight. Rinse well, then drain. Put them in a pressure cooker with 4 cups water. Cook at high pressure for 15–20 minutes or until tender. Drain.

If using unsoaked chickpeas, cook at high pressure for 30–40 minutes or until tender.

This salad is delicious served as a lunch or light dinner, or even as a breakfast dish.

Chickpea, zucchini, and mint salad with garlic toasts

Preparation time: 15 minutes
Cooking time: 5 minutes
Serves 4

8 thin slices sourdough baguette (see tips)

Olive oil spray, for coating

1 garlic clove, peeled and halved

2 large zucchini, trimmed

2 teaspoons white balsamic vinegar

2 teaspoons olive oil

2 teaspoons finely grated lemon zest

14-oz can chickpeas, drained and rinsed (see tips)

1 roasted red bell pepper, thinly sliced (see tips)

2¾ oz (75 g) crumbled soft goat's cheese

¼ cup baby or micro mint leaves

4 poached eggs (optional)

1 Preheat a grill pan over high heat. Spray the baguette slices lightly with olive oil. Grill for 2 minutes each side or until lightly charred. Rub one side of each slice with the cut side of the garlic clove. Set aside.

2 Peel long ribbons from the zucchini using a vegetable peeler, stopping when you reach the seeds. Place the zucchini ribbons in a large bowl (discard the seeds or reserve for another use) and add the vinegar, olive oil, and lemon zest. Set aside to marinate for 5 minutes.

3 Add the chickpeas, bell pepper, goat's cheese, and half the mint and toss to combine. Divide the salad between four plates. Top each with a poached egg (if desired), garnish with the remaining mint, and serve with the garlic toasts.

tips For a gluten-free version of this dish, substitute gluten-free bread for the sourdough baguette.

You can replace the canned chickpeas with 1⅓ cups cooked chickpeas.

To roast your own bell pepper, cut a large bell pepper in half and remove the seeds and membranes. Put the halves on a baking tray and roast at 400°F for 20–25 minutes, or until the skin starts to blacken. Transfer to a small bowl, cover with plastic wrap, and set aside to steam for 15 minutes. Carefully peel off the skin, and discard.

Honey spice
roasted chickpeas

(see recipe page 23)

Roasted sweet potato
and cashew hummus

(see recipe page 22)

vegan • gluten-free

Roasted sweet potato adds sweetness to this version of hummus, and cashews add a delicious creaminess. Try serving it on crackers, as a healthy alternative to mayonnaise in sandwiches, or with vegetable sticks for a nutritious snack.

Roasted sweet potato and cashew hummus

Preparation time: 15 minutes
Cooking time: 25 minutes
Makes 2 cups

1 small sweet potato (about 10½ oz), peeled and coarsely chopped

Olive oil spray, for coating

14-oz can chickpeas, drained and rinsed (see tips)

2 tablespoons roasted unsalted cashews, coarsely chopped

1 tablespoon tahini

1 garlic clove, crushed

½ teaspoon ground cumin

½ teaspoon sweet paprika, plus extra to garnish

Pinch of dried chili flakes (optional)

¼ cup olive oil, plus extra to garnish

1 tablespoon lemon juice

1 Preheat the oven to 400°F. Line a small baking tray with parchment paper. Place the sweet potato on the prepared tray and spray lightly with olive oil to coat. Bake for 25 minutes or until golden and tender. Set aside to cool.

2 Process the chickpeas, cashews, tahini, garlic, spices, and sweet potato in a food processor until well combined. Add the olive oil, lemon juice, and 2–3 tablespoons warm water. Process until smooth and creamy. Season to taste with sea salt and freshly ground black pepper. Serve drizzled with extra olive oil and sprinkled with extra paprika.

tips You can replace the canned chickpeas with 1⅓ cups cooked chickpeas. When you're cooking dried chickpeas for this or any other hummus recipe, process the cooked chickpeas while they're still hot. This way, the skins will disintegrate and the hummus will be smooth.

Hummus will keep in an airtight container in the refrigerator for up to 4 days.

« pictured pages 20–21

vegetarian • dairy-free • gluten-free

Roasted chickpeas make a delicious and super-healthy snack on the go. Low GI and naturally gluten-free and dairy-free, they make a great low-fat substitute for roasted nuts. They're lunchbox-friendly too. For a vegan version, replace the honey with rice malt syrup.

Honey spice roasted chickpeas

Preparation time: 5 minutes
(plus 20 minutes draining)
Cooking time: 30 minutes
Serves 2

14-oz can chickpeas, drained and
rinsed (see tips)
1 tablespoon single-origin
pure floral honey
1 teaspoon ground cinnamon
Pinch of freshly grated nutmeg
Olive oil spray, for coating

1 Preheat the oven to 400°F. Line a baking tray with parchment paper. Put the chickpeas on a plate lined with paper towel and set aside for 20 minutes to remove excess moisture.

2 Combine the chickpeas, honey, cinnamon, and nutmeg in a medium bowl. Stir to coat the chickpeas in the honey. Place on the prepared tray and spray lightly with olive oil to coat.

3 Roast for 30 minutes, gently shaking the tray every 10 minutes. The chickpeas should be dark golden and slightly crisp. Remove from the oven and set aside to cool. The chickpeas will continue to become crisp as they cool.

tips You can replace the canned chickpeas with 1⅓ cups cooked chickpeas.

It's essential to remove as much moisture from the chickpeas as possible so that they become crisp when cooked. They will keep in an airtight container for 2 days.

« pictured page 21

vegetarian • gluten-free (see tips)

Try serving these falafel wrapped in flat bread with tabouleh, or break them into chunks and toss them through a salad for a healthy and filling vegetarian meal. Chickpeas are a wonderful vegetarian source of protein and packed with insoluble fiber – great for digestive health.

Falafel with tomato and radish salad

Preparation time: 20 minutes
(plus 30 minutes chilling)
Cooking time: 15 minutes
Serves 4

2 x 14-oz cans chickpeas, drained and rinsed (see tips)

1/3 cup mint leaves, coarsely chopped

1/3 cup flat-leaf (Italian) parsley leaves, coarsely chopped

1 1/2 tablespoons lightly toasted pine nuts

1 egg white

1 garlic clove, crushed

1 1/2 teaspoons ground cumin

1 teaspoon ground coriander

1/2 teaspoon baking soda

All-purpose flour, for dusting (see tips)

1 tablespoon olive oil

Plain (natural) yogurt, to serve

Grilled flat bread, to serve (see tips)

TOMATO AND RADISH SALAD

1 cup grape tomatoes, halved

4 radishes, trimmed and thinly sliced

1/4 cup mint leaves

3 scallions, trimmed and thinly sliced

2 teaspoons olive oil

1 Process the chickpeas, mint, parsley, pine nuts, egg white, garlic, spices, and baking soda in a food processor until almost smooth. Dust your hands with flour and shape the mixture into 20 small oval falafels. Place on a tray, cover with plastic wrap, and refrigerate for 30 minutes to firm.

2 Meanwhile, to make the tomato and radish salad, combine the tomatoes, radishes, mint, and scallions in a medium bowl. Drizzle with the olive oil, season to taste with sea salt and freshly ground black pepper, and toss gently to combine. Set aside.

3 Heat the oil in a large non-stick frying pan over medium–high heat. Cook the falafels, in two batches, for 4 minutes each side, or until golden brown and cooked through. Serve with tomato and radish salad, yogurt, and flat bread.

tips You can replace the canned chickpeas with 2 2/3 cups cooked chickpeas. For a gluten-free version of this dish, use gluten-free flour and gluten-free flat bread.

Chickpeas make this soup extremely filling and nutritious. It's substantial enough to serve as a main meal.

Chickpea, lemon, and Swiss chard soup

Preparation time: 20 minutes
Cooking time: 30 minutes
Serves 4

1 tablespoon olive oil

1 large onion, finely chopped

1 fennel bulb, trimmed, finely chopped

2 celery stalks, diced

3 garlic cloves, crushed

1 teaspoon finely grated lemon zest

½ teaspoon dried chili flakes

4 vine-ripened tomatoes, diced

2 x 14-oz cans chickpeas, drained and rinsed (see tips)

4 cups low-sodium vegetable stock

½ bunch Swiss chard, trimmed and leaves shredded

Lemon juice, to taste

1 Heat the olive oil in a large saucepan over medium heat. Add the onion, fennel, and celery and cook, stirring, for 6–7 minutes or until softened. Add the garlic, lemon zest, and chili flakes and cook, stirring, for 1 minute or until fragrant.

2 Add the tomatoes and cook, stirring, for 2–3 minutes. Add the chickpeas and stock and bring to the boil. Reduce the heat to low and simmer for 15 minutes.

3 Stir in the Swiss chard and simmer for 2 minutes or until wilted. Season to taste with lemon juice, sea salt, and freshly ground black pepper.

tips For a gluten-free version, use gluten-free vegetable stock.

You can replace the canned chickpeas with $2\frac{2}{3}$ cups cooked chickpeas.

This soup is suitable to freeze. Place it in airtight containers, cool completely, cover, and freeze for up to 2 months.

dairy-free • gluten-free

Chickpeas make a delicious, speedy, low-GI alternative to mashed potatoes. Prepared in this way they have a nutty taste and a creamy texture.

Piri piri chicken with smashed chickpeas

Preparation time: 20 minutes
(plus 30 minutes marinating)
Cooking time: 15 minutes
Serves 4

2 x 9-oz chicken breasts, fat trimmed

1 tablespoon olive oil

Finely grated zest and juice of 1 lemon

1 teaspoon finely grated lime zest

2 garlic cloves, crushed

½ teaspoon dried chili flakes

½ teaspoon ground turmeric

Arugula leaves, to serve

SMASHED CHICKPEAS

2 teaspoons olive oil

1 small red onion, finely chopped

2 garlic cloves, crushed

1 teaspoon ground cumin

1 teaspoon sweet paprika

2 x 14-oz cans chickpeas, drained and rinsed (see tip)

½ cup low-sodium chicken stock

1 tablespoon lemon juice, or to taste

1 Cut each chicken breast horizontally through the middle to give 4 thin fillets. Combine the olive oil, lemon zest and juice, lime zest, garlic, chili flakes, and turmeric in a shallow glass or ceramic dish. Add the chicken and turn to coat. Cover and refrigerate for 30 minutes to marinate.

2 Meanwhile, to make the smashed chickpeas, heat the olive oil in a medium saucepan over medium heat. Add the onion and cook, stirring, for 5 minutes or until softened. Add the garlic, cumin, and paprika and cook, stirring, for 1 minute or until fragrant. Add the chickpeas and stock. Simmer for 2–3 minutes. Transfer the chickpea mixture to a food processor and process until smooth. Add lemon juice to taste and season with sea salt and freshly ground black pepper. Return to a clean saucepan and keep warm.

3 Preheat a grill pan or barbecue plate over high heat. Drain excess marinade from the chicken. Grill the chicken for 3 minutes each side, or until lightly charred and cooked through. Thickly slice. Serve with the smashed chickpeas and arugula.

tip You can replace the canned chickpeas with 2⅔ cups cooked chickpeas.

dairy-free • gluten-free

This stew also makes a delicious vegetarian meal. Simply omit the lamb and serve with grilled haloumi, or flat bread.

Chickpea stew with rosemary and lemon grilled lamb

Preparation time: 20 minutes
(plus 30 minutes marinating)
Cooking time: 25 minutes
Serves 4

1 tablespoon olive oil

1 tablespoon lemon juice

2 teaspoons rosemary, coarsely chopped

1 teaspoon finely grated lemon zest

12 French-trimmed lamb cutlets

Baby spinach leaves, to serve

CHICKPEA STEW

2 teaspoons olive oil

1 red onion, finely chopped

2 celery stalks, trimmed and diced

2 garlic cloves, crushed

1 teaspoon sweet paprika

1 tablespoon unsalted tomato paste (concentrated purée)

2 x 14-oz cans chickpeas, drained and rinsed (see tips)

14-oz can diced tomatoes

1 Combine the oil, lemon juice, rosemary, and lemon zest in a shallow glass or ceramic dish. Add the lamb cutlets and turn to coat. Cover and refrigerate for 30 minutes to marinate.

2 Meanwhile, to make the chickpea stew, heat the olive oil in a large saucepan over medium heat. Add the onion and celery and cook, stirring, for 6–7 minutes or until softened. Add the garlic and paprika and cook, stirring, for 1 minute or until fragrant. Stir in the tomato paste and cook for 1 minute. Then add the chickpeas, cherry tomatoes, and ⅓ cup water. Bring to the boil, reduce the heat to low, and simmer, stirring occasionally, for 10 minutes.

3 Preheat a grill pan or barbecue plate over high heat. Drain excess marinade from the cutlets. Grill the cutlets for 2 minutes each side for medium, or until cooked to your liking. Cover loosely with foil and set aside to rest for 2 minutes.

4 Season the chickpeas to taste with sea salt and freshly ground black pepper. Serve with the cutlets and baby spinach leaves.

tips You can replace the canned chickpeas with 2⅔ cups cooked chickpeas.

The stew is suitable to freeze without the cutlets or spinach leaves. Place it in an airtight container, cool completely, cover, and freeze for up to 2 months.

**Massaman
chickpea curry**

(see recipe page 34)

**Raisin, coconut, and
cilantro flat breads**

(see recipe page 35)

vegetarian • dairy-free • gluten-free (see tips)

Nutty chickpeas are delicious combined with spices and sweet coconut milk – you won't even notice there isn't any meat in this hearty curry. You can use reduced-fat coconut milk if you wish, but the sauce may split a little.

Massaman chickpea curry

Preparation time: 20 minutes
Cooking time: 1 hour 15 minutes
Serves 4

1 cup dried chickpeas, soaked overnight and drained (see tips)
2 teaspoons vegetable oil
2 onions, thinly sliced
¼ cup Massaman curry paste
2 cinnamon sticks
2 cardamom pods, lightly crushed
2 fresh bay leaves
9½ fl oz can coconut milk
1 cup vegetable stock
2 carrots, peeled and chopped into chunks
12 oz (2–3 medium) potatoes, peeled and chopped into chunks
Cilantro leaves, to garnish
Steamed Asian greens, to serve

1 Place the chickpeas in a large saucepan and cover with cold water. Bring to the boil, then reduce the heat to low, and simmer for 45 minutes–1 hour or until tender. Drain and set aside.

2 Heat the oil in a large saucepan or wok over medium heat. Add the onion and cook, stirring, for 3–4 minutes or until softened. Add the curry paste, cinnamon, cardamom, and bay leaves and cook, stirring, for 1–2 minutes or until fragrant.

3 Add the coconut milk, stock, cooked chickpeas, and carrots and bring to the boil. Reduce the heat to low, cover, and simmer for 10 minutes. Add the potatoes, cover, and simmer for 15–20 minutes or until the potatoes are tender.

4 Serve garnished with cilantro, with steamed Asian greens.

tips For a gluten-free version, use gluten-free curry paste and vegetable stock.

You can use canned chickpeas in this recipe. You will need two 14-oz cans chickpeas, drained and rinsed. Add with the potatoes in step 3.

This curry is suitable to freeze. Place it in airtight containers, cool completely, cover, and freeze for up to 2 months.

« pictured page 32

dairy-free • gluten-free

Chickpea flour has a wonderful nutty taste once it's cooked, and it's extremely nutritious. Like all gluten-free breads, these flat breads are not as robust as those made with wheat flour, so handle them gently.

Raisin, coconut, and cilantro flat breads

Preparation time: 15 minutes
(plus 1 hour resting)
Cooking time: 15 minutes
Makes 4

1 cup chickpea flour (besan)
1 tablespoon olive oil, plus extra for brushing
2 tablespoons cilantro leaves, finely chopped
2 tablespoons dried unsweetened coconut
1½ tablespoons raisins

1 Sift the chickpea flour into a large bowl. Gradually add ¾ cup water, whisking until well combined, then continue to whisk for 1–2 minutes or until smooth. Whisk in the olive oil. Cover and set aside to rest for 1 hour.

2 Stir in the cilantro, coconut, raisins, and a large pinch of sea salt. Heat a medium non-stick frying pan over medium–high heat and brush with a little extra olive oil. Ladle in a quarter of the batter (about ¼ cup) and tilt the pan to spread the batter out to a 6-inch diameter circle.

3 Cook for 2 minutes or until bubbles start to appear on the surface. Carefully flip, and cook for a further 1–2 minutes or until golden and cooked through. Transfer to a plate and keep warm. Repeat with the remaining batter to make 4 flat breads.

tip These flat breads are best eaten straight away.

« pictured page 33

dairy-free • gluten-free (see tips)

Chickpeas add a nutty taste, texture, and body to this delicious cake, which doesn't contain any oil or butter. It will keep in an airtight container for up to 3 days.

Mandarin, pistachio, and chickpea cake

Preparation time: 20 minutes
Cooking time: 1 hour 50 minutes
Serves 12

3 mandarins, unpeeled

1¼ cups shelled unsalted pistachios

14-oz can chickpeas, drained and rinsed (see tips)

¾ cup granulated sugar

4 eggs

½ cup all-purpose flour (see tips)

1 teaspoon baking powder

Icing (confectioners') sugar, for dusting

1 Place the mandarins in a large saucepan, cover with cold water, and bring to the boil, then drain. Cover with cold water again, return to the boil, then reduce the heat to low, and simmer for 45 minutes, adding a little more water to the pan as necessary. Drain mandarins and set aside to cool.

2 Preheat the oven to 325°F. Lightly grease an 8½-inch round cake pan and line it with parchment paper.

3 Cut the mandarins into quarters and remove the seeds (discard). Coarsely chop 1 tablespoon of the pistachios and reserve for the garnish, then process the remaining pistachios in a food processor to fine crumbs. Remove; set aside. Add the chickpeas to the food processor and process to fine crumbs. Add the mandarins and process until smooth.

4 Use an electric mixer to whisk the sugar and eggs in a large bowl until thick. Add the mandarin mixture and fold in until well combined, then add the ground pistachios, flour, and baking powder and stir until well combined. Spoon the batter into the prepared pan and smooth the surface with the back of the spoon.

5 Bake for 50 minutes or until a skewer inserted into the center comes out with a few moist crumbs. If the cake browns too quickly, cover the top loosely with foil. Set aside to cool for 20 minutes, then carefully remove from the pan, and cool completely on a wire rack. Serve dusted with icing sugar and garnished with the reserved chopped pistachios.

tips For a gluten-free version, replace the flour with gluten-free all-purpose flour.

You can replace the canned chickpeas with 1⅓ cups cooked chickpeas.

white beans

white beans

Cannellini beans, navy beans, and lima beans are collectively referred to as white beans, and their many similarities make them interchangeable in most bean-based recipes. Along with many other bean varieties, they all share the species name *Phaseolus vulgaris*. Like all beans, the white beans are high in protein and fiber, have virtually no fat, are high in folate, vitamins and minerals, and have a low glycemic index, making them highly nutritious.

cannellini beans

CANNELLINI BEANS ARE prominent in Italian cuisine, particularly in the recipes of Tuscany.

They are creamy white in color and have a distinctive kidney shape. Their firm smooth texture and mild nut-like flavor have made them popular in many classic Italian recipes, such as minestrone soup.

Cooked, they have a fluffy and creamy texture, making them ideal in soups, braises, and salads, and as a substitute for potato to make a creamy mash. They can also be added to baked goods such as cookies or cakes, replacing some of the butter or flour content, or both. This adds a good dose of protein and fiber, increasing overall nutrition.

Cannellini beans are available dried and canned. The flavor and texture of canned beans are not quite as good as those of dried beans, but the canned version is a very handy pantry staple. Look for those with minimal or no added salt.

Uncooked cannellini beans, like lima beans and red kidney beans, contain a toxic compound that can cause digestive upsets if the beans are not prepared properly. It is essential to boil the beans to make them safe to eat. Slow cookers may not reach the temperatures required, so, to be safe, boil dried cannellini beans on the stovetop for 10 minutes before adding them to the slow cooker.

Pressure cookers operate at higher temperatures than slow cookers, and beans cooked in them don't need any special treatment.

Canned cannellini beans are fine to use straight from the can.

Cooking instructions

Stovetop

Soak 1 cup dried cannellini beans in cold water overnight. Rinse well, then drain. Put them in a large saucepan, add water to cover the beans by 2 inches, and bring to the boil. Reduce the heat to low and simmer for 45 minutes–1 hour or until tender. Drain.

Pressure cooker

Soak 1 cup dried cannellini beans in cold water overnight. Rinse well, then drain. Put them in a pressure cooker with 4 cups water. Cook at high pressure for 5–10 minutes or until tender.

If using unsoaked cannellini beans, cook at high pressure for 20–25 minutes or until tender.

NUTRITION	PER 100 G (3½ OZ) COOKED CANNELLINI BEANS
Energy	96 cal
Protein	6.2 g
Fat	0.6 g
Saturated fat	0.2 g
Carbohydrate	12.2 g
Dietary fiber	6.4 g
Calcium	46 mg
Folate	81 µg
Magnesium	30 mg
Potassium	260 mg

navy beans

DURING THE 19TH CENTURY, navy beans (also known as haricot beans) were the staple diet of the United States navy, hence their name. Many classic American bean dishes are based on navy beans, including the all-time favorite, baked beans. Even today, they are the beans used in commercially made canned baked beans.

Smaller than cannellini beans, navy beans are creamy white in color, and they have a dense texture when cooked. Their mild flavor means they absorb other flavors beautifully, and they are best teamed with stronger-tasting ingredients such as tomatoes, onions, and garlic.

Nutritionally, navy beans are slightly higher in folate and iron than other beans, and they have a high saponin content. Saponins are phytochemicals that have been associated with health benefits such as reducing the risk of certain cancers and reducing blood cholesterol.

Cooking instructions

Stovetop
Soak 1 cup dried navy beans in cold water overnight. Rinse well, then drain. Put them in a large saucepan, add water to cover the beans by 2 inches, and bring to the boil. Reduce the heat to low and simmer for 1–1½ hours or until tender. Drain.

Pressure cooker
Soak 1 cup dried navy beans in cold water overnight. Rinse well, then drain. Put them in a pressure cooker with 4 cups water. Cook at high pressure for 10–15 minutes or until tender. Drain.

If using unsoaked beans, add 2 cups water and cook at high pressure for 20–30 minutes or until tender.

NUTRITION	PER 100 G (3½ OZ) COOKED NAVY BEANS
Energy	110 cal
Protein	8.2 g
Fat	0.7 g
Saturated fat	0.1 g
Carbohydrate	12.6 g
Dietary fiber	8.8 g
Calcium	57 mg
Folate	140 µg
Magnesium	49 mg
Potassium	340 mg

lima beans

LIMA BEANS, ALSO KNOWN as butter beans, originated some 8000 years ago in South America. They are much larger than cannellini beans and navy beans, but they have a similar mild, buttery flavor and creamy texture.

Nutritionally, lima beans are high in protein, almost fat-free, and rich in dietary fiber, folate, and magnesium. Their high soluble and insoluble fiber levels are associated with many health benefits, including improved digestive health, steady blood sugar levels, and lowered cholesterol.

Lima beans are common in the cuisines of South America, where they are often boiled and served as a side dish, seasoned with salt, pepper, and butter. They are also used in casseroles, stews, salads, and soups.

Lima beans are available dried, canned, and occasionally fresh. When purchasing dried lima beans, choose beans that are smooth, not split or cracked. Cracked beans tend to fall apart during the cooking process.

Raw lima beans, like cannellini beans and red kidney beans, contain a toxic compound that can cause digestive upsets if the beans are not prepared properly. It is essential to boil the beans to make them safe to eat. Slow cookers may not reach the temperatures required, so, to be safe, boil dried lima beans on the stovetop for 10 minutes before adding them to the slow cooker.

Pressure cookers operate at higher temperatures than slow cookers, and beans cooked in them don't need any special treatment.

Canned lima beans are fine to use straight from the can.

Cooking instructions

Stovetop

Soak 1 cup dried lima beans in cold water overnight. Rinse well, then drain. Put them in a large saucepan, add water to cover by 2 inches, and bring to the boil. Reduce the heat to low and simmer for 45 minutes–1 hour or until tender. Drain.

Pressure cooker

Soak 1 cup dried lima beans in cold water overnight. Rinse well, then drain. Put them in a pressure cooker with 4 cups water. Cook at high pressure for 5–10 minutes or until tender.

If using unsoaked lima beans, cook at high pressure for 12–15 minutes or until tender.

NUTRITION	PER 100 G (3½ OZ) COOKED LIMA BEANS
Energy	85 cal
Protein	6.4 g
Fat	0.3 g
Saturated fat	0.1 g
Carbohydrate	10.2 g
Dietary fiber	5.3 g
Folate	83 µg
Magnesium	35 mg
Potassium	350 mg

These pancakes have a light and fluffy texture and are healthy enough that you can happily serve them to your family any day of the week for breakfast — they won't even taste the beans! The cannellini beans are packed with protein and dietary fiber, and the oats are a whole grain, full of beta glucan soluble dietary fiber, which keeps you feeling full for longer.

Oat pancakes with berries

Preparation time: 15 minutes
Cooking time: 25 minutes
Makes 8

½ cup rolled oats

14-oz can cannellini beans, drained and rinsed (see tips)

2 eggs

1 tablespoon maple syrup, plus extra to serve

1 teaspoon pure vanilla extract

½ cup all-purpose flour (see tips)

2 teaspoons baking powder

¾ cup milk

1½ tablespoons butter, melted

Fresh berries, to serve

Plain (natural) yogurt, to serve

1 Process the oats in a food processor until finely ground. Transfer to a large bowl.

2 Process the cannellini beans in the food processor until smooth. Add the eggs, maple syrup, and vanilla and process until well combined. Add to the bowl with the oats.

3 Sift the flour and baking powder over the oat mixture, add the milk, and whisk to a smooth batter. Set aside for 10 minutes.

4 Heat a large non-stick frying pan over medium–high heat, then brush the pan with a little of the melted butter. Ladle ¼ cup of the batter into the pan. Cook for 2 minutes or until bubbles appear on the surface. Turn and cook the other side for 1 minute or until light golden. Transfer to a plate and keep warm while you make the remaining pancakes. Serve with fresh berries, a dollop of yogurt, and a drizzle of maple syrup.

tips You can replace the canned cannellini beans with 1⅓ cups cooked cannellini beans.

These pancakes can be made with gluten-free all-purpose flour.

For a dairy-free version, replace the milk with soy, rice, or almond milk, and replace the butter with oil.

Best baked beans

(see recipe page 48)

dairy-free • gluten-free (see tips)

Nothing beats home-made baked beans. This recipe makes a big batch, but it will keep covered in the refrigerator for up to 4 days. It is worth taking the time to use dried beans, because for this dish they have a better texture after baking than the canned ones.

Best baked beans

Preparation time: 20 minutes
(plus overnight soaking)
Cooking time: 2 hours 10 minutes
Serves 6

1½ cups dried navy (haricot) beans, soaked in cold water overnight and drained

1 tablespoon olive oil

1 large onion, finely chopped

1 carrot, peeled and finely chopped

2 celery stalks, finely chopped

3½ oz pancetta or bacon, trimmed and diced

3 garlic cloves, thinly sliced

1 teaspoon smoked paprika

2 fresh bay leaves

2 tablespoons unsalted tomato paste (concentrated purée)

14-oz can crushed tomatoes

1 tablespoon Worcestershire sauce

1 tablespoon maple syrup

2 teaspoons dijon mustard

1 Place the beans in a large saucepan and cover with cold water. Bring to the boil, reduce the heat to low, and simmer for 1 hour or until just tender. Drain and set aside.

2 Preheat the oven to 325°F. Heat the oil in a large flameproof casserole dish over medium–high heat. Add the onion, carrot, celery, and pancetta and cook, stirring, for 5–6 minutes or until softened. Add the garlic, paprika, and bay leaves and cook, stirring, for 1 minute or until fragrant.

3 Add the tomato paste and cook, stirring, for 1 minute. Add the tomatoes, beans, Worcestershire sauce, maple syrup, mustard, and 2 cups water. Cover and bake for 1½–2 hours or until thick and tender. Serve.

tips For a gluten-free version, choose a gluten-free Worcestershire sauce.

Baked beans are suitable to freeze. Place them in airtight containers and cool completely. Cover and freeze for up to 2 months.

« pictured pages 46–47

vegan • gluten-free (see tips)

Avocado is full of good fats, and deliciously creamy, but it is high in calories. Supplementing it with white beans is a great way to add fiber and an extra serving of vegetables, reducing the overall calorie count for a healthy and filling breakfast.

White beans, avocado, and wilted tomatoes on toast

Preparation time: 10 minutes
Cooking time: 10 minutes
Serves 4

1 cup grape tomatoes, halved

Olive oil spray, for coating

14-oz can cannellini or lima beans, drained and rinsed (see tips)

1 teaspoon lemon juice, or to taste

Pinch of dried chili flakes (optional)

1 firm ripe avocado, peeled, stone removed, coarsely chopped

2 tablespoons flat-leaf (Italian) parsley, coarsely chopped

4 slices wholegrain or sourdough bread, toasted

1 Preheat the oven to 350°F. Line a large baking tray with parchment paper. Place the tomatoes cut-side up on the prepared tray and spray with olive oil. Roast for 10 minutes or until wilted.

2 Meanwhile, put the beans, lemon juice, and chili flakes in a large bowl. Mash coarsely with a fork, leaving some texture. Add the avocado and parsley and gently stir to combine. Season to taste with sea salt and freshly ground black pepper.

3 To serve, spoon the bean mixture onto the toast slices and top with the wilted tomatoes.

tips For a gluten-free version, use gluten-free bread.

You can replace the canned beans with 1½ cups cooked cannellini or lima beans.

If you are short on time, skip roasting the tomatoes.

vegetarian • gluten-free

Cauliflower combined with egg and parmesan makes a fantastic gluten-free alternative to traditional pizza bases.

Cauliflower crust pizza with white beans, squash, and cherry tomatoes

Preparation time: 25 minutes
Cooking time: 55 minutes
Makes 2 pizzas

½ butternut squash (about 1¾ lb), peeled, seeded and cut into ⅝-inch dice

Olive oil spray, for coating

1½ tablespoons olive oil

1 tablespoon finely chopped mint, plus ¼ cup mint leaves, to serve

2 teaspoons finely chopped rosemary

1 teaspoon finely grated lemon zest, plus extra to serve

⅓ cup finely grated mozzarella

14-oz can lima beans, drained and rinsed (see tips)

1 cup grape tomatoes, halved

2 tablespoons finely grated parmesan cheese

¼ cup flat-leaf (Italian) parsley leaves

CAULIFLOWER CRUST

1 large head cauliflower, trimmed and cut into florets

2 eggs, lightly beaten

⅓ cup finely grated parmesan cheese

1 garlic clove, crushed

1 Preheat the oven to 425°F. Line a baking tray and two large pizza trays with parchment paper. Place the squash on the prepared baking tray and spray with olive oil to coat. Roast for 25 minutes or until golden and tender.

2 Meanwhile, to make the cauliflower crust, process cauliflower in batches in a food processor until finely chopped. Transfer to a large microwave-safe bowl and cover with plastic wrap. Microwave on high for 8 minutes or until just tender (see tips). Drain, return to bowl, and cool completely. Stir in eggs, parmesan, and garlic. Divide mixture in half and press each portion into an 8½-inch circle approximately ⅛ inch thick on a lined pizza tray. Spray with olive oil spray and bake for 15 minutes or until edges are golden.

3 Combine oil, chopped herbs, and zest in a bowl. Brush crusts with oil mixture, sprinkle with mozzarella, and top with beans, tomatoes, roasted squash, and parmesan. Bake pizzas, rotating trays halfway through cooking, for 12 minutes or until golden.

4 Meanwhile, combine the mint leaves, extra lemon zest, and parsley in a small bowl. Scatter over the pizzas and serve.

tips Microwaving the cauliflower gives the best results for this recipe. It's not necessary to add any water, but it's important to cover the cauliflower so it steams. Alternatively, you can steam the cauliflower, covered, over simmering water on the stovetop for 8 minutes or until just tender, then drain and cool.

You can replace the canned lima beans with 1⅓ cups cooked lima beans.

Abington Free Library
1030 Old York Road
Abington, PA 19001-4530

**Bean and cauliflower
soup with basil oil**

(see recipe page 54)

**Ribollita with
parmesan chili croutons**

(see recipe page 55)

This soup is quick, easy, and so delicious. The white beans not only add a good dose of protein, fiber and B vitamins, they also give a deliciously creamy texture and body to the soup.

Bean and cauliflower soup with basil oil

Preparation time: 20 minutes
Cooking time: 20 minutes
Serves 4

1 tablespoon olive oil

1 large leek, white part only, thinly sliced

2 stalks celery, diced

2 garlic cloves, crushed

1 small head cauliflower, trimmed and cut into florets

3 cups low-sodium vegetable stock

14-oz can cannellini beans, drained and rinsed (see tips)

2 tablespoons freshly grated parmesan cheese

BASIL OIL
1/2 cup basil leaves, plus extra to garnish

1/4 cup olive oil

1 Heat the olive oil in a large saucepan over medium heat. Add the leek and celery and cook, stirring, for 6–7 minutes or until softened. Add the garlic and cook, stirring, for 1 minute or until fragrant.

2 Add the cauliflower, stock, and beans. Bring to the boil, reduce the heat to low, and simmer for 10 minutes or until the cauliflower is tender. Set aside to cool slightly.

3 Meanwhile, to make the basil oil, place the basil and oil in a food processor or blender. Process until smooth. Strain through a fine sieve (discard solids) and set aside.

4 Blend the cauliflower mixture in batches until smooth and creamy. Return the soup to a clean saucepan and heat over medium heat until warmed through. Stir in the parmesan and season to taste with sea salt and freshly ground black pepper.

5 Serve the soup with a drizzle of basil oil, garnished with basil leaves.

tips For a gluten-free version, use gluten-free vegetable stock. You can replace the canned cannellini beans with 1 1/3 cups cooked cannellini beans.

This soup is suitable to freeze. Place it in airtight containers, cool completely then cover and freeze for up to 2 months.

If you don't have time to make the basil oil, serve the soup with a small dollop of ready-made basil pesto.

« **pictured page 52**

Ribollita is a rustic Tuscan soup; the name literally means "reboiled." It is often served the day after it's made, when the flavors have had time to develop. The recipe is versatile, but traditionally it includes white beans, vegetables, and leftover bread. This version contains a little prosciutto, but for a vegetarian version, simply omit it. The white beans are a wonderful source of plant protein and dietary fiber.

Ribollita with parmesan chili croutons

**Preparation time: 25 minutes
(plus overnight soaking)
Cooking time: 1 hour
Serves 4**

1¼ cups dried cannellini beans, soaked in cold water overnight and drained

1 tablespoon olive oil

1 large onion, finely chopped

2 celery stalks, trimmed and diced

2 slices prosciutto, diced (optional)

3 garlic cloves, crushed

1 teaspoon fennel seeds, lightly crushed

5 cups low-sodium vegetable or chicken stock

1 bunch lacinato (Tuscan) kale, trimmed and coarsely chopped (see tips)

PARMESAN CHILI CROUTONS

4 slices sourdough bread, torn into bite-sized pieces

Olive oil spray, for coating

2 tablespoons finely grated parmesan cheese

¼ teaspoon dried chili flakes

1 Place the beans in a large saucepan and cover with cold water. Bring to the boil, then reduce the heat to medium and simmer for 45 minutes–1 hour or until just tender. Drain and set aside.

2 Meanwhile, preheat the oven to 350°F. Heat the olive oil in a large saucepan over medium heat. Add the onion, celery, and prosciutto (if using) and cook, stirring, for 5 minutes or until softened. Add the garlic and fennel seeds and cook, stirring, for 30 seconds or until fragrant.

3 Add the stock, cooked beans, and kale. Bring to the boil, then reduce the heat to low and simmer for 15 minutes. Season to taste with sea salt and freshly ground black pepper.

4 Meanwhile, to make the parmesan chili croutons, place the bread on a large baking tray lined with parchment paper. Spray with olive oil, then sprinkle with the parmesan and chili flakes. Bake for 10–15 minutes or until golden and crisp.

5 Serve the soup scattered with the croutons.

tips If you do not have lacinato kale, you can use Swiss chard.

The soup is suitable to freeze without the croutons. Place it in airtight containers, cool completely, cover, and freeze.

« pictured page 53

dairy-free • gluten-free

This is the perfect summer salad — light, healthy, and easy to cook on the barbecue. The cannellini beans make it filling and substantial enough for dinner. Feel free to use white beans of any sort.

Grilled seafood salad with beans, dill, and lemon dressing

Preparation time: 20 minutes
Cooking time: 15 minutes
Serves 4

2 tablespoons olive oil

1 long red chili, seeded and finely chopped

2 garlic cloves, crushed

1 lb baby calamari, cleaned, tentacles reserved

16 large peeled raw prawns (shrimp), deveined, tails intact

2 tablespoons coarsely chopped dill

1½ tablespoons lemon juice

1 teaspoon finely grated lemon zest

Pinch of granulated sugar

14-oz can cannellini beans, drained and rinsed (see tips)

16 asparagus spears, trimmed

Olive oil spray, for coating

3 cups loosely packed baby arugula leaves

Lemon wedges, to garnish

1 Combine 1 tablespoon of the olive oil, the chili, and the garlic in a shallow glass or ceramic dish. Score the inside of the calamari bodies and cut into 1½-inch squares. Add them to the olive oil mixture along with the reserved tentacles and prawns and stir to coat. Cover and set aside in the refrigerator to marinate for 1–2 hours.

2 Combine the remaining olive oil, dill, lemon juice, lemon zest, and sugar in a large bowl. Add the cannellini beans and stir to coat.

3 Preheat a grill pan or barbecue plate over high heat. Spray the asparagus lightly with olive oil. Grill the asparagus for 1 minute each side or until lightly charred and tender. Add to the bean mixture.

4 Grill the calamari and prawns in batches for 1–2 minutes each side or until lightly charred and just cooked (be careful not to overcook the calamari or it will become tough). Remove and add to the bean mixture. Add the arugula and gently toss to combine. Serve immediately with lemon wedges.

tip You can replace the canned cannellini beans with 1⅓ cups cooked cannellini beans.

The slightly aniseed flavor of fennel is perfect with salty capers and sweet roasted tomatoes. This salad is simple to prepare and is perfect for lunch or a light dinner.

Tuna, white bean, fennel, tomato, and caper salad

Preparation time: 20 minutes
Cooking time: 25 minutes
Serves 4

1½ **cups cherry tomatoes, halved**

Olive oil spray, for coating

7 **oz green beans, trimmed**

1 **fennel bulb, trimmed and thinly sliced**

2 **teaspoons lemon juice**

14-oz **can cannellini beans, drained and rinsed (see tips)**

6½-oz **can tuna in olive oil, drained and flaked**

⅓ **cup flat-leaf (Italian) parsley leaves**

CAPER DRESSING

1 **tablespoon salted baby capers, rinsed and finely chopped**

1 **tablespoon olive oil**

1 **tablespoon white balsamic vinegar**

2 **teaspoons lemon juice**

1 Preheat the oven to 300°F. Line a large baking tray with parchment paper. Put the tomatoes cut-side up on the prepared tray. Spray with olive oil and season to taste with sea salt and freshly ground black pepper. Roast for 25 minutes or until wilted. Set aside.

2 Cook the green beans in a saucepan of boiling water until just tender. Refresh under cold running water. Drain.

3 Place the fennel in a large bowl, drizzle with the lemon juice, and toss to combine. Add the roasted tomatoes, green beans, cannellini beans, tuna, and parsley.

4 To make the caper dressing, whisk the capers, olive oil, balsamic vinegar, and lemon juice together in a small bowl. Add to the salad, gently toss to combine, and serve.

tips You can replace the canned cannellini beans with 1⅓ cups cooked cannellini beans.

If you're short of time, you can roast the tomatoes at 350°F for only 10 minutes. Roasting them for longer at a lower temperature intensifies their sweetness and flavor.

Lima beans combine beautifully with peas to make a delicious smooth and creamy mash, packed with dietary fiber and protein. For a vegan version you can omit the ricotta.

Lima bean, ricotta, and pea mash

Preparation time: 5 minutes
Cooking time: 10 minutes
Serves 4

1½ cups frozen baby green peas
2 teaspoons olive oil
1 shallot, finely chopped
2 garlic cloves, crushed
14-oz can lima beans, drained and rinsed (see tip)
⅓ cup fresh ricotta

1 Cook the peas in a large saucepan of boiling water for 3–4 minutes or until tender. Drain well and set aside.

2 Heat the oil in a clean saucepan over medium heat. Add the shallot and cook, stirring, for 3 minutes or until softened. Add the garlic and cook for 30 seconds or until fragrant. Add the lima beans, peas, and 2 tablespoons water and simmer for 1 minute.

3 Transfer to a food processor, add the ricotta and process until smooth. Season to taste with sea salt and freshly ground black pepper, then serve.

tip You can replace the canned lima beans with 1⅓ cups cooked lima beans.

Curries don't come much healthier than this one. Lima beans contain virtually no fat, and they're rich in protein, fiber, magnesium, and folate. Their creamy texture and mild taste are perfect for absorbing all the delicious flavors of the spices.

Fragrant bean and sweet potato curry with curry leaves

Preparation time: 20 minutes
(plus overnight soaking)
Cooking time: 1½ hours
Serves 4

1⅓ cups dried lima beans, soaked in cold water overnight and drained (see tips)

1 tablespoon vegetable oil

12 fresh curry leaves

2 teaspoons brown mustard seeds

2 onions, coarsely chopped

3 garlic cloves, crushed

1¼-inch piece ginger, peeled and finely grated

1 teaspoon ground cumin

2 long green chilies, seeded and finely chopped

4 vine-ripened tomatoes, coarsely chopped

1 cup low-sodium vegetable stock

1 small sweet potato (about 10½ oz), peeled and cut into ¾-inch chunks

1⅔ cups baby spinach leaves

1 Place the beans in a large saucepan and cover with cold water. Bring to the boil, then reduce the heat to medium and simmer for 45 minutes–1 hour or until just tender. Drain and set aside.

2 Heat the oil in a large saucepan over medium heat. Add the curry leaves and mustard seeds and cook, stirring, for 1 minute. Add the onion and cook, stirring, for 3–4 minutes or until softened. Add the garlic, ginger, cumin, and chilies and cook, stirring, for 1 minute or until fragrant.

3 Add the tomatoes and cook for 2–3 minutes or until thick. Add the beans, stock, and ½ cup water. Bring to the boil, then reduce the heat to low, cover, and simmer for 10 minutes.

4 Add the sweet potato, cover, and cook for a further 10 minutes or until the sweet potato is tender. Stir in the spinach leaves and serve.

tips For a gluten-free version, use gluten-free vegetable stock.

You can replace the dried lima beans with 2 x 14-oz cans lima beans, drained and rinsed. Omit step 1 and add the beans in step 3.

The curry is suitable to freeze without the spinach. Put it in airtight containers, cool completely, cover, and freeze.

Macadamia and fig cookies

(see recipe page 64)

Vanilla almond cakes

(see recipe page 65)

Beans can be used in some baked goods to replace some of the butter and flour. This helps lower the GI and reduce the fat content of these sweet treats.

Macadamia and fig cookies

Preparation time: 15 minutes
Cooking time: 15 minutes
Makes 30

½ cup canned or cooked lima beans, rinsed and drained

1 egg

1 tablespoon maple syrup

⅔ cup firmly packed brown sugar

⅓ cup unsalted butter, softened slightly

1 teaspoon pure vanilla extract

1½ cups all-purpose flour

1 teaspoon ground cinnamon

½ teaspoon ground ginger

½ teaspoon baking powder

½ cup dried figs, coarsely chopped

½ cup macadamia nuts, coarsely chopped

2 tablespoons finely chopped crystallized ginger

1 Preheat the oven to 350°F. Line a large baking tray with parchment paper.

2 Process the beans, egg, and maple syrup in a food processor until smooth.

3 Use an electric mixer to beat the sugar, butter, and vanilla until pale and creamy. Add the bean mixture and beat until well combined. Sift the flour, spices, and baking powder together. Slowly beat the flour mixture into the butter mixture, then stir in the figs, macadamia nuts, and crystallized ginger.

4 Place tablespoons of the mixture about 2 inches apart on the prepared tray. Flatten each cookie slightly using a lightly floured fork. Bake for 15 minutes or until lightly golden around the edges and cooked through. Transfer to a wire rack to cool completely. Repeat with remaining mixture.

tips The cookies will keep in an airtight container for 3–4 days.

You can replace the lima beans with cannellini beans.

《 **pictured page 62**

These cupcakes are so simple to make, and they taste amazing. They have a lovely moist texture, and you cannot taste the beans. They are packed with protein and dietary fiber and contain no added oil or butter.

Vanilla almond cakes

Preparation time: 10 minutes
Cooking time: 20 minutes
Makes 10

14-oz can cannellini beans, drained and rinsed (see tips)

3 eggs

1¼ cups almond meal

½ cup coconut sugar

2 teaspoons baking powder

2 teaspoons pure vanilla extract

Sifted unsweetened cocoa powder, to garnish

1 Preheat the oven to 350°F. Line 10 holes of a 12-hole standard muffin tin with paper cases.

2 Process beans in a food processor until smooth, scraping down the sides of the bowl if necessary. Add the eggs one at a time and process until smooth. Add the almond meal, sugar, baking powder, and vanilla. Process again until well combined.

3 Divide the mixture between the paper cases. Bake for 15–20 minutes or until light golden and firm to touch. Transfer to a wire rack to cool for 5 minutes, remove from the tin, and set aside on the wire rack to cool completely. Serve dusted with cocoa powder.

tips You can replace the canned cannellini beans with 1⅓ cups cooked cannellini beans.

These cupcakes are suitable to freeze. Cool completely then wrap individually in plastic wrap and freeze for up to 1 month.

« **pictured page 63**

soy beans & adzuki beans

soy beans

SOY BEANS ARE NATIVE to Southeast Asia and date back more than 5000 years. Like all legumes, they are rich in protein, but one unique feature sets soy beans apart from other legumes: their high oil content, which is extracted and used to make cooking oil. Soy beans are now an important crop globally for both protein and oil.

Soy beans are an incredibly versatile legume. The immature beans can be eaten fresh (in this state they're often referred to as edamame), and the dried mature beans can be soaked and used as a high-protein legume. Soy beans can also be processed to make an array of soy products, including soy flour, tofu, soy milk, and textured vegetable protein (TVP), and fermented foods such as soy sauce, miso paste, and tempeh.

The proliferation of soy products stems from the fact that soy protein is heat-stable, or able to withstand high temperatures during processing. The beans are also popular for their impressive complete protein profile: they contain all nine essential amino acids, which means they match animal products as a protein source. This property has made soy beans and their products a popular and essential food for vegetarians and vegans throughout the world.

Soy beans are also a good source of B vitamins, potassium, and zinc, and low in saturated fat. They contain certain isoflavones that have been linked to various health benefits, including easing menopausal symptoms in women, and reducing the risk of osteoporosis and certain cancers.

Edamame are bright green and can be purchased fresh in the pod, although they can be tricky to find in this form. They're also available flash-frozen from the frozen vegetable section of supermarkets and Asian grocery stores. They're delicious served as a snack with simply a drizzle of oil and a sprinkle of sea salt. Or they can be removed from the pod and used as a salad vegetable, added to soup or pasta, or even made into pesto.

Mature soy beans can be purchased dried or canned. Dried soy beans need to be soaked and then cooked in plenty of water until tender. Canned soy beans are already cooked, and simply require rinsing and draining before adding to soups, curries, or salads.

Cooking instructions

Stovetop
Soak 1 cup dried soy beans in cold water overnight. Rinse well and drain. Put them in a large saucepan, add water to cover the beans by 2 inches, and bring to the boil. Reduce the heat to low and simmer for 1–1½ hours or until tender. Drain.

Pressure cooker
Soak 1 cup dried soy beans in cold water overnight. Rinse well and drain. Put them in a pressure cooker with 4 cups water. Cook at high pressure for 10–15 minutes or until tender.

If using unsoaked soy beans, cook at high pressure for 25–35 minutes.

NUTRITION	PER 100 G (3½ OZ) COOKED DRIED SOY BEANS
Energy	146 cal
Protein	13.5 g
Fat	7.7 g
Saturated fat	1.1 g
Carbohydrate	1.3 g
Dietary fiber	7.2 g
Calcium	76 mg
Zinc	1.6 mg
Magnesium	71 mg
Potassium	420 mg

adzuki beans

ADZUKI BEANS, *VIGNA ANGULARIS*, also known
as azuki beans, are native to Asia and are cultivated
extensively throughout East Asia and the Himalayas.
These small oval red beans have a distinctive white
ridge along one side, and are available dried or canned.

Adzuki beans can be added to salads, curries, and
stews. They have a slightly sweet and nutty taste that
marries well with most flavors, especially Asian flavors.

Boiled with sugar to make a sweet red bean paste,
the beans are used as a filling in Japanese and
Chinese sweets, dumplings, and sweet cakes, or as
a topping for waffles, pastries, buns, and cookies.
Sweetened red bean soups, often served topped with
coconut cream or sweetened condensed milk, are
popular in China and Japan.

Adzuki beans are a high-protein, high-fiber, low-
fat plant food source. Rich in the minerals calcium,
phosphorus, and magnesium, they make a wonderful
addition to any diet. Their high soluble fiber content
can help to stabilize cholesterol levels, improve
digestive health, and keep you feeling full for longer.

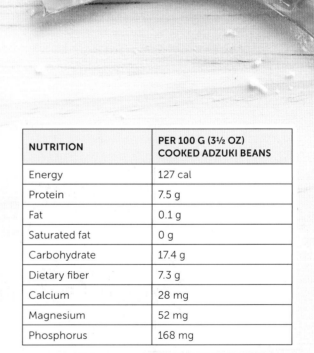

Cooking instructions

Stovetop
Soak 1 cup dried adzuki beans in cold water
overnight. Rinse and drain. Put them in a large
saucepan, add water to cover the beans by 2 inches,
and bring to the boil. Reduce the heat to low and
simmer for 30–45 minutes or until tender. Drain.

Pressure cooker
Soak 1 cup dried adzuki beans in cold water
overnight. Rinse and drain. Put them in a pressure
cooker with 4 cups water. Cook at high pressure for
5–10 minutes or until tender. Drain.

If using unsoaked adzuki beans, cook at high
pressure for 15–20 minutes or until tender.

NUTRITION	PER 100 G (3½ OZ) COOKED ADZUKI BEANS
Energy	127 cal
Protein	7.5 g
Fat	0.1 g
Saturated fat	0 g
Carbohydrate	17.4 g
Dietary fiber	7.3 g
Calcium	28 mg
Magnesium	52 mg
Phosphorus	168 mg

The soy bean is one of the few plant foods that is a complete protein; that is, it contains all the essential amino acids. These burgers, with their combination of soy beans and quinoa, are packed with protein and fiber.

Quinoa bean burgers with fresh beet slaw

Preparation time: 25 minutes
Cooking time: 25 minutes
Serves 4

1½ tablespoons olive oil

1 onion, finely chopped

1 tablespoon korma curry paste

⅓ cup quinoa, rinsed and drained

14-oz can soy beans, drained and rinsed (see tips)

1 small carrot, peeled and finely grated

2 tablespoons finely chopped mixed soft herbs, such as parsley, mint, and cilantro

2 tablespoons sunflower seeds

⅓ cup quinoa flakes

4 burger buns, halved and toasted

2 tablespoons hummus

Baby arugula, to serve

BEET SLAW

1 tablespoon red wine vinegar

2 teaspoons honey

1 teaspoon wholegrain mustard

2 beets, peeled and coarsely grated

1 small green apple, cored and coarsely grated

1 Heat 2 teaspoons of the olive oil in a medium saucepan over medium heat. Cook the onion, stirring, for 5 minutes or until softened. Add the curry paste and cook, stirring, for 30 seconds or until fragrant. Add the quinoa and ⅔ cup water and bring to the boil. Reduce the heat to low, cover, and simmer for 10–12 minutes or until the water has evaporated and the quinoa is just tender. Set aside to cool completely.

2 Mash the soy beans in a large bowl, leaving a little texture. Add the quinoa, carrot, herbs, and sunflower seeds and mix until well combined. Shape into 4 patties. Place the quinoa flakes on a large plate and press each patty into the flakes to coat on all sides.

3 Heat the remaining olive oil in a large non-stick frying pan over medium heat. Cook the burgers for 3 minutes each side or until golden and crisp.

4 Meanwhile to make the beet slaw, combine the red wine vinegar, honey, and mustard in a medium bowl. Add the beets and apple and stir until well combined.

5 Spread the burger buns with hummus. Fill each bun with arugula, a burger, and beet slaw and serve.

tips For a gluten-free version, use gluten-free burger buns.

It is important to cook the quinoa until all the water has evaporated to ensure the burgers are not too wet.

You can replace the canned soy beans with 1⅓ cups cooked soy beans or another type of canned legume, such as mixed beans, chickpeas, or cannellini beans.

This kale pesto is a light and healthy variation on the standard basil mix. As well as adding a flavor kick to the soup, it's bursting with vitamin C, beta carotene, folate, calcium, and iron.

Bean, barley, and vegetable soup with kale pesto

Preparation time: 20 minutes
Cooking time: 45 minutes
Serves 4

1 tablespoon olive oil

1 large onion, finely chopped

2 celery stalks, diced

1 large carrot, peeled and diced

3½ oz pancetta, diced (optional)

2 garlic cloves, crushed

3 cups low-sodium chicken or vegetable stock

14-oz can diced tomatoes

⅓ cup pearl barley, rinsed and drained

¼ small cabbage (about 14 oz), trimmed and coarsely shredded

14-oz can adzuki beans, drained and rinsed (see tips)

KALE PESTO

1½ cups trimmed and chopped kale

¼ cup finely grated parmesan cheese

2 tablespoons pine nuts, lightly toasted

1 teaspoon finely grated lemon zest

2 garlic cloves, coarsely chopped

2 tablespoons olive oil

1 tablespoon lemon juice

1 To make the kale pesto, place the kale, parmesan, pine nuts, lemon zest, and garlic in a food processor or blender and process until finely chopped. Add the olive oil, lemon juice, and 2 tablespoons hot water and process until a paste forms, adding a little more hot water if necessary. Season to taste with sea salt and freshly ground black pepper. Makes ½ cup.

2 Heat the olive oil in a large saucepan over medium heat. Add the onion, celery, carrot, and pancetta (if desired) and cook, stirring, for 6–7 minutes or until softened. Add the garlic and cook, stirring, for 30 seconds or until fragrant.

3 Add the stock, tomatoes, barley, and 2 cups water. Bring to the boil, then reduce the heat to low and simmer for 20 minutes. Add the cabbage and simmer for 10 minutes or until the barley is tender.

4 Add the adzuki beans and simmer for 5 minutes or until heated through. Season to taste with sea salt and freshly ground black pepper. Serve topped with a dollop of kale pesto.

tips You can replace the canned adzuki beans with 1⅓ cups cooked adzuki beans.

Leftover kale pesto can be used as a spread on bread or crackers, or tossed through pasta. It will keep in an airtight container in the refrigerator for up to 4 days.

Freekeh is wheat that is picked when the grain is young and green. It's higher in nutrients such as protein, calcium, iron, and zinc than mature wheat, and higher in fiber too. You can substitute cracked freekeh in salads where you would typically use brown rice, bulgur, or couscous.

Freekeh and bean salad with almonds and raisins

Preparation time: 15 minutes
Cooking time: 20 minutes
Serves 4

1 cup cracked freekeh

7 oz green beans, trimmed and sliced

1 bunch broccolini, trimmed and cut into 1¼-inch lengths

14-oz can adzuki beans, drained and rinsed (see tips)

¼ small red cabbage (about 14 oz), trimmed and finely shredded

¼ cup raw almonds, coarsely chopped

2 tablespoons raisins

2 tablespoons snipped chives

2 tablespoons coarsely chopped mint

1 tablespoon olive oil

1 tablespoon apple cider vinegar

2 teaspoons lemon juice

1 teaspoon honey (optional)

1 Cook the freekeh in a large saucepan of lightly salted boiling water for 12–15 minutes or until al dente. Rinse under cold running water, then drain well, squeezing out as much water as possible. Transfer to a large bowl.

2 Meanwhile, cook the green beans and broccolini in a saucepan of boiling water until just tender. Drain, refresh under cold running water, and drain again.

3 Add the green beans, broccolini, adzuki beans, cabbage, almonds, raisins, chives, and mint to the bowl with the freekeh.

4 Whisk together the olive oil, vinegar, lemon juice, and honey (if desired) in a small bowl. Add to the salad, gently toss to combine, and serve.

tips For a vegan version, omit the honey.

You can replace the canned adzuki beans with 1⅓ cups cooked adzuki beans.

Add the dressing just before serving, because the acid in the dressing will eventually start to discolor the green vegetables.

» pictured pages 210–211

dairy-free

Adzuki beans are popular in Asian cooking, especially Japanese cooking. Their creamy texture and slight sweetness work well with flavors such as soy, ginger, and chili.

Sesame-crusted tuna with adzuki beans, soba noodles, and spinach

Preparation time: 15 minutes
Cooking time: 10 minutes
Serves 4

7 oz dried soba noodles

8 asparagus spears, trimmed and thinly sliced

14-oz can adzuki beans, drained and rinsed (see tips)

$1^2/_3$ cups baby spinach leaves

3 scallions, trimmed and thinly sliced

2 tablespoons low-sodium soy sauce

1 tablespoon mirin

1 teaspoon sesame oil

1 teaspoon finely grated ginger

1 long red chili, seeded and finely chopped

2 tablespoons white or black sesame seeds

1 nori sheet, crushed

2 x 9-oz tuna steaks, skin removed

2 teaspoons olive oil

1 Cook the noodles in a large saucepan of lightly salted boiling water according to the package instructions or until al dente. Add the asparagus for the last minute of cooking time. Drain, refresh under cold running water, and drain again. Transfer to a large bowl. Add the adzuki beans, spinach, and scallions. Set aside.

2 Whisk together the soy, mirin, sesame oil, ginger, and chili in a small bowl. Add to the noodles and gently toss to combine. Set aside.

3 Scatter the sesame seeds and nori on a large plate. Press a piece of tuna into the sesame seed mixture, then turn to coat on both sides. Repeat with the remaining tuna steak.

4 Heat the oil in a large non-stick frying pan over high heat. Add the tuna and cook for 1–2 minutes each side for rare, or until cooked to your liking. Thickly slice.

5 Divide the noodle salad between serving plates and top with tuna slices. Serve immediately.

tips You can replace the canned adzuki beans with $1^1/_3$ cups cooked adzuki beans.

Salmon makes a good alternative to tuna in this recipe. You will need 2 x 9-oz salmon fillets; cook them for 2–3 minutes each side for rare.

Edamame, prawn, and crisp wonton salad

(see recipe page 78)

Edamame with chili salt

(see recipe page 79)

This salad makes a fresh and light entrée, or, if served with some crusty bread, a light lunch.

Edamame, prawn, and crisp wonton salad

Preparation time: 25 minutes
Cooking time: 5 minutes
Serves 4

3 cups fresh or frozen edamame (soy beans)

2 tablespoons peanut oil

8 wonton wrappers

20 large peeled cooked prawns (shrimp), deveined, tails intact

2 cups picked watercress leaves

1 firm ripe avocado, stone removed, peeled and thinly sliced

¼ cup mint leaves

1 red Asian shallot, thinly sliced

NAM JIM DRESSING

2 tablespoons lime juice

3 teaspoons fish sauce

2 teaspoons brown sugar

2 teaspoons finely grated ginger

2 long red chilies, seeded and finely chopped

1 garlic clove, crushed

1 Cook the edamame in a saucepan of boiling water for 2 minutes or until just tender. Drain, refresh under cold running water, and drain again. Remove the beans from the pods (discard the pods) and set aside.

2 Heat the oil in a large frying pan over medium–high heat. Cook the wonton wrappers in batches for 30 seconds each side or until golden and crisp. Transfer to a plate lined with paper towel. Set aside.

3 To make the nam jim dressing, place all the ingredients in a small bowl and stir until the sugar has dissolved.

4 Break the wonton wrappers into large pieces. Combine the shelled edamame, wonton pieces, prawns, watercress, avocado, mint, and shallot in a large bowl. Divide between serving plates. Drizzle with the dressing and serve immediately.

tips The dressing can be made a day ahead and stored in an airtight container in the refrigerator.

You can replace the watercress with another peppery green such as baby arugula.

« *pictured pages 76–77*

Edamame make a delicious and healthy snack. They need to be removed from their outer pods before eating, so serve them with a bowl for the leftover pods.

Edamame with chili salt

Preparation time: 5 minutes
Cooking time: 5 minutes
Serves 4

½ teaspoon dried chili flakes

½ teaspoon sea salt

2 ½ cups fresh or frozen edamame (soy beans)

1 tablespoon low-sodium tamari

½ teaspoon sesame oil

1 Combine the chili flakes and salt in a small bowl and set aside.

2 Cook the edamame in a saucepan of boiling water for 2 minutes or until just tender. Drain.

3 Transfer the edamame to a serving bowl. Drizzle with the tamari and sesame oil. Sprinkle with the chili salt. Serve immediately.

tips For a gluten-free version, use gluten-free tamari.

Fresh soy beans (edamame) can be tricky to find. Frozen soy beans are available all year round, and can be found in the frozen vegetable section of supermarkets and Asian food stores.

« pictured page 76

The soy beans in this hearty braise reduce the amount of meat needed, and they're nutritious too. Soy beans are high in fiber, a good source of plant protein, and, unlike most legumes, rich in omega 3 fatty acids.

Oven-braised pork with soy beans, eggplant, and chili bean sauce

Preparation time: 20 minutes
(plus overnight soaking)
Cooking time: 1 hour 40 minutes
Serves 4

1½ tablespoons peanut oil

1 lb skinless pork belly, trimmed of excess fat and cut into ¾-inch chunks (see tips)

1 large red onion, finely chopped

2 celery stalks, diced

2 garlic cloves, crushed

4 star anise

1 cinnamon stick

1 cup dried soy beans, soaked in cold water overnight and drained

2 tablespoons chili bean sauce (see tips)

2 tablespoons unsalted tomato paste (concentrated purée)

1 tablespoon low-sodium soy sauce

1 eggplant, trimmed and cut into ⅝-inch dice

Steamed Asian greens, to serve

1 Preheat the oven to 325°F. Heat 2 teaspoons of the oil in a large flameproof casserole dish over high heat. Add half the pork and cook, turning occasionally, for 2–3 minutes or until golden. Remove and set aside. Repeat with 2 more teaspoons of the oil and the remaining pork.

2 Return the casserole dish to medium heat. Add the onion and celery and cook, stirring, for 3 minutes or until softened. Add the garlic, star anise, and cinnamon and cook, stirring, for 1 minute or until fragrant.

3 Return the pork to the casserole dish. Add the soy beans, chili bean sauce, tomato paste, soy sauce, and 2 cups water and bring to the boil. Cover, transfer to the oven, and bake for 1 hour.

4 Meanwhile, heat 1 teaspoon of the oil in a large non-stick frying pan over high heat. Add half the eggplant and cook, stirring, for 2–3 minutes or until browned. Remove and set aside. Repeat with the remaining 1 teaspoon of oil and the remaining eggplant. Add the eggplant to the pork mixture. Cover and return to the oven for a further 30 minutes or until the pork and beans are tender. Serve with steamed Asian greens.

tips You could replace the pork belly with diced pork shoulder or leg.

Chili bean sauce is a reddish-brown sauce made from fermented soy beans and chilies. It's available from Asian supermarkets and Asian grocers. If you prefer a milder dish, you can substitute black bean and garlic sauce, which is available from most supermarkets.

gluten-free

Double choc bean brownies

Preparation time: 20 minutes
Cooking time: 35 minutes
Makes 16

Adzuki beans add richness and body as well as a good dose of dietary fiber and protein to these brownies. Adding beans means you don't need to use as much oil or butter, and the brownies are naturally gluten-free.

5½ oz dark chocolate, coarsely chopped

⅓ cup macadamia oil, or other mildly flavored nut or seed oil such as sunflower or safflower oil

14-oz can adzuki beans, drained and rinsed (see tip)

2 eggs

1 teaspoon pure vanilla extract

2 tablespoons unsweetened cocoa powder, plus extra for dusting

½ cup firmly packed brown or coconut sugar

⅓ cup almond or hazelnut meal

1 Preheat the oven to 325°F. Lightly grease an 8-inch square cake pan and line the base with parchment paper.

2 Put half of the chocolate and all of the macadamia oil in a heatproof bowl over a saucepan of gently simmering water. Stir until melted and smooth. Set aside to cool.

3 Process the adzuki beans in a food processor until smooth. Add the eggs and vanilla and process until well combined. Transfer to a large bowl.

4 Stir the chocolate mixture into the bean mixture, then sift the cocoa over the mixture and stir until well combined. Stir in the sugar, nut meal, and remaining chopped chocolate.

5 Pour the mixture into the prepared pan. Bake for 30 minutes or until just firm when lightly pressed. Set aside to cool in the pan before cutting into squares. Serve dusted with extra cocoa.

tip You can replace the adzuki beans with 1⅓ cups cooked adzuki beans, red kidney beans, or black beans.

peas

peas

Green peas, snow peas, and sugarsnap peas are all members of the plant family Fabaceae and therefore classed as legumes, but they are somewhat unusual among legumes in that they are typically sold and prepared as fresh or frozen vegetables, rather than in a dried form.

green peas

GREEN PEAS, *PISUM SATIVUM*, also known as garden peas, are grown in many parts of the world. Modern cultivars originated from wild peas that grew in the Mediterranean basin thousands of years ago.

Pea pods are 2–3¼ inches long; inside are smooth round green seeds (peas), attached to one side of the pod. The pods are harvested before maturity and the sweet green peas are extracted. Small young peas are sweeter than older peas. After picking, the sugar in peas starts to convert to starch.

Green peas are sold fresh in the pod, already shelled, snap-frozen, or canned. They can be eaten raw (young peas are especially delicious eaten this way), steamed, or boiled. It is best to cook peas briefly and to add as little water as possible, to minimize loss of nutrients and flavor.

The tender leafy shoots from young pea plants, known as pea shoots, are also edible, and can be used as a salad green or in stir-fries.

Incredibly versatile, peas can be added to salads, curries, pastas, risottos, soups, casseroles, and pies, or even turned into mash. Green peas make a wonderful side dish, and their flavor partners beautifully with fresh mint, feta, lemon zest, or bacon.

Green peas are extremely nutritious. As well as being a good source of protein, they are rich in pectin, a type of soluble fiber linked to the regulation of blood cholesterol levels. They're high in vitamin C, an antioxidant linked with boosting immunity, and vitamin A, which is essential for eye health. They are also a useful source of zinc, iron, and niacin.

Cooking instructions

Place freshly shelled peas in a steamer over a saucepan of boiling water. Cover and steam for 3–4 minutes or until just tender. Alternatively, cook peas in a saucepan of boiling water for 3–4 minutes, then drain.

Frozen peas need less cooking time than fresh ones, only 2–3 minutes.

NUTRITION	PER 100 G (3½ OZ) COOKED GREEN PEAS
Energy	63 cal
Protein	4.8 g
Fat	0.4 g
Saturated fat	0.1 g
Carbohydrate	5.5 g
Dietary fiber	5.5 g
Vitamin C	14 mg
Folate	63 µg
Iron	1.1 mg

snow peas & sugarsnap peas

SNOW PEAS AND SUGARSNAP PEAS are two varieties of peas specifically bred to be eaten intact, pod and all. Snow peas consist of flat, wide pods containing small flat seeds. The pods of sugarsnap peas look similar to the pods of regular green peas, but narrower. The peas inside are round.

Both snow peas and sugarsnaps are crisp, and taste sweet and delicious. Look for snow peas and sugarsnaps with crunchy pods and a strong green color; avoid any that are limp or pale.

To prepare them for cooking, simply trim the ends and remove the fibrous string that runs the length of the pod. Snow peas and sugarsnaps can be eaten raw, lightly steamed, or boiled.

Popular in Asian cuisine, they're often used in stir-fries, Asian soups, and salads. They also make a wonderful side dish drizzled with olive oil and topped with toasted nuts, crumbled feta, or chili and garlic.

Pea pods are rich in insoluble fiber, which aids digestive health and can relieve constipation. Snow peas and sugarsnaps are not quite as rich in protein as green peas, but they're higher in vitamin C and a good source of potassium, niacin, folate, and beta carotene (a precursor to vitamin A).

Cooking instructions

Place trimmed sugarsnap peas or snow peas in a steamer over a saucepan of boiling water. Cover and steam for 2 minutes or until just tender. Alternatively, cook them in a saucepan of boiling water for 1–2 minutes. Drain.

NUTRITION	PER 100 G (3½ OZ) COOKED SUGARSNAP PEAS	PER 100 G (3½ OZ) COOKED SNOW PEAS
Energy	21 cal	45 cal
Protein	1.5 g	3.6 g
Fat	0.2 g	0.3 g
Saturated fat	0 g	0 g
Carbohydrate	2.2 g	5.6 g
Dietary fiber	2.5 g	3.3 g
Vitamin C	13 mg	46.8 mg
Folate	33 µg	15.9 µg

Cooking instructions

WHOLE DRIED PEAS

Stovetop

Soak 1 cup whole dried peas in cold water overnight. Rinse and drain. Place in a large saucepan, add cold water to cover by 2 inches, and bring to the boil. Reduce the heat to low and simmer for 1 hour or until tender, skimming scum. Drain.

Pressure cooker

Soak 1 cup whole dried peas in cold water overnight. Rinse and drain. Place in a pressure cooker with 4 cups water. Cook at high pressure for 10 minutes or until tender.

If using unsoaked peas, cook at high pressure for 15–20 minutes.

SPLIT PEAS

Stovetop

Split peas cook quite quickly without soaking, although soaking has the advantage of reducing the amount of scum that rises to the surface during cooking. It also reduces the cooking time somewhat.

Rinse and drain the peas. Place in a large saucepan, add cold water to cover by 2 inches, and bring to the boil. Reduce the heat to low and simmer for 30–45 minutes or until tender, skimming scum. Drain.

Pressure cooker

Without soaking, put the split peas in a pressure cooker with 4 cups water. Cook at high pressure for 5–10 minutes or until tender. Drain.

dried & split peas

DRIED AND SPLIT PEAS are a special variety of peas known as field peas. Generally too tough to be eaten fresh, they are grown specifically to be dried. Dried peas were a staple of medieval cuisine, and they form the basis of split pea soup.

Whole dried peas can be roasted, seasoned, and eaten as a snack (wasabi peas are a popular example). They can also be used as a substitute for fresh peas in curries and stews. Mushy peas, the popular accompaniment to meat pies and (in the UK) fish and chips, are rehydrated and mashed dried peas.

Split peas are dried peas that have had their tough outer skin removed and have been split in half. Split peas have more flavor than whole dried peas and require less cooking time. Both green and yellow varieties are widely available; the yellow ones have a more delicate flavor. Most recipes for traditional pea and ham soup use split peas, as do many Indian recipes for dal.

Dried peas are packed with soluble and insoluble fiber. Soluble fiber has been linked to reduced cholesterol levels; insoluble fiber can assist digestive disorders such as irritable bowel syndrome and constipation, and help to stabilize blood sugar levels.

NUTRITION	PER 100 G (3½ OZ) COOKED SPLIT PEAS
Energy	87 cal
Protein	6.6 g
Fat	0.4 g
Saturated fat	0 g
Carbohydrate	9.1 g
Dietary fiber	8.3 g
Folate	65 µg
Potassium	140 mg

This versatile frittata is just the thing for breakfast on the run or a packed lunch.
Or serve it with plenty of salad leaves and some crusty bread for a light dinner.
For a vegetarian version, omit the salmon and add some crumbled feta.

Pea, asparagus, ricotta, and smoked salmon frittata

Preparation time: 15 minutes
Cooking time: 25 minutes
Serves 4

Olive oil spray, for greasing
1 cup fresh or frozen baby green peas
8 asparagus spears, trimmed and thinly sliced
8 eggs
¾ cup fresh ricotta
¼ cup milk
1 tablespoon snipped chives
1 teaspoon finely grated lemon zest
3½ oz smoked salmon, diced
Pea shoots or baby spinach leaves, to serve

1 Preheat the oven to 350°F. Lightly spray an 8-inch x 12-inch non-stick baking pan with oil and line the base with parchment paper.

2 Cook the peas in a saucepan of boiling water for 2–3 minutes or until just tender, adding the asparagus for the last minute of cooking time. Refresh under cold running water and drain.

3 Put the eggs, ½ cup of the ricotta, milk, chives, and lemon zest in a medium bowl, season to taste with sea salt and freshly ground black pepper, and whisk to combine. Add the asparagus, peas, and salmon and stir to combine. Pour the mixture into the prepared pan. Dollop the remaining ricotta over the top.

4 Bake the frittata for 20–25 minutes or until golden and puffed. Remove from the oven and set aside to cool slightly before carefully removing from the pan. Serve warm or at room temperature with pea shoots or baby spinach leaves.

tip Frittata is delicious served warm or at room temperature.

» pictured page 92

vegetarian • *gluten-free*

Regular peas are eaten without their pods, whereas sugarsnaps and snow peas are eaten whole, pods included. This salad makes the most of their crisp texture and fresh taste. Buttermilk, despite its name, is low in fat, but it has a lovely creamy texture and a slight tang, making it perfect for a salad dressing.

Three-pea salad with buttermilk herb dressing

Preparation time: 15 minutes
Cooking time: 5 minutes
Serves 4

1 cup shelled fresh or frozen baby peas

7 oz snow peas, trimmed

7 oz sugarsnap peas, trimmed

4 small radishes, trimmed and thinly sliced

¼ cup mint leaves

¼ cup flat-leaf (Italian) parsley leaves

BUTTERMILK HERB DRESSING

¼ cup buttermilk

1 tablespoon finely snipped chives

1 tablespoon finely chopped dill or flat-leaf (Italian) parsley

2 teaspoons lemon juice

1 teaspoon finely grated lemon zest

1 Put the baby peas in a steamer over a saucepan of boiling water, cover, and steam for 3–4 minutes or until just tender. Refresh under cold running water, drain, and transfer to a large bowl. Steam the snow peas and sugarsnap peas in the same way, cooking for 2 minutes or until just tender. Refresh, drain, and transfer to the bowl with the baby peas. Add the radishes, mint, and parsley and toss gently to combine.

2 To make the buttermilk herb dressing, whisk all the ingredients in a small bowl until combined.

3 Arrange the salad on a serving platter and drizzle with the dressing. Serve immediately.

» **pictured page 93**

Pea, asparagus,
ricotta, and smoked
salmon frittata

(see recipe page 90)

Three-pea salad with buttermilk herb dressing

(see recipe page 91)

Split peas are peas that have been shelled, dried, hulled, and then split in half. They have more flavor and take less time to cook than whole dried peas.

Split pea and ham hock soup with mint relish

Preparation time: 15 minutes
(plus 2 hours soaking)
Cooking time: 1 hour 40 minutes
Serves 6

1 tablespoon olive oil

1 large onion, finely chopped

2 carrots, finely chopped

3 celery stalks, diced

2 garlic cloves, crushed

3 fresh bay leaves

2 thyme sprigs

1 ham hock (about 1¾ lb)

1⅔ cups yellow split peas, soaked in cold water for 2 hours, drained

MINT RELISH

2 tablespoons finely chopped mint

2 tablespoons finely chopped flat-leaf (Italian) parsley

Zest of ½ lemon, thinly sliced

1 Heat the oil in a large saucepan over medium heat. Add the onion, carrot, and celery and cook, stirring, for 6–7 minutes or until softened. Add the garlic, bay leaves, and thyme and cook, stirring, for 1 minute or until fragrant.

2 Add the ham hock, split peas, and 8 cups water. Bring to the boil over high heat. Reduce the heat to low and simmer, partially covered, for 1½ hours or until the peas are tender and the soup has thickened. Remove the ham hock and set aside to cool slightly. Shred the meat from the hock (discard the skin and bones) and return the shredded meat to the soup.

3 To make the mint relish, put all the ingredients in a small bowl and stir to combine. Set aside.

4 Reheat the soup over medium heat. Season to taste with freshly ground black pepper and serve with a spoonful of mint relish.

tips If you're short of time you can omit soaking the peas, but they will take a little longer to cook.

This soup is suitable to freeze. Put it in airtight containers, cool completely, cover, and freeze for up to 2 months.

This dish is light, fresh, healthy, and on the table in less than 20 minutes. Stir-frying is a great method of cooking peas — being extremely quick, it helps minimize loss of nutrients.

Steamed lemongrass fish with stir-fried peas

Preparation time: 15 minutes
Cooking time: 15 minutes
Serves 4

4 x 5½-oz firm white fish fillets (such as cod or hake)

1 lemongrass stem, pale part only, thinly sliced

1¼-inch piece ginger, peeled and cut into thin matchsticks

1 teaspoon peanut or macadamia oil

7 oz snow peas, trimmed

5½ oz sugarsnap peas, trimmed

4 scallions, trimmed and cut into 1¼-inch lengths

2 garlic cloves, thinly sliced

1 tablespoon low-sodium tamari

1 teaspoon sesame oil

1 Line a large steamer with parchment paper. Place the fish fillets in the steamer and sprinkle with the lemongrass and ginger. Put the steamer over a saucepan of simmering water, ensuring the base is not touching the water. Cover and steam for 6–7 minutes or until the fish is just cooked and flakes easily when tested with a fork at the thickest part.

2 Meanwhile, heat the oil in a large wok over high heat. Stir-fry the snow peas and sugarsnap peas for 2 minutes. Add the scallions and garlic and stir-fry for 1–2 minutes or until the vegetables are just tender. Add the tamari and sesame oil and toss to combine.

3 Serve the steamed fish with the stir-fried peas.

tip For a gluten-free version, use gluten-free tamari.

Cauliflower makes a fantastic substitute for rice in this take on traditional fried rice. Low in carbohydrates, providing an extra serving of vegetables, packed with cancer-fighting antioxidants, and full of flavor, it is a winner on all levels.

Cauliflower fried "rice" with peas

Preparation time: 20 minutes
Cooking time: 15 minutes
Serves 4

1 small head cauliflower, trimmed and cut into florets

1 tablespoon peanut oil

9 oz chicken breast, thinly sliced

16 peeled raw prawns (shrimp), tails intact, deveined

1 onion, finely chopped

1 carrot, peeled and cut into thin matchsticks

2 garlic cloves, crushed

2 teaspoons finely grated ginger

7 oz snow peas, trimmed and sliced

1 cup shelled fresh or frozen green peas

2 tablespoons low-sodium tamari

2 teaspoons hot chili sauce, plus extra to serve

2 tablespoons coarsely chopped cilantro

Lime halves, to serve

1 Process the cauliflower in batches in a food processor until it is about the size of rice grains. Don't over-process it; aim to retain some texture. Set aside.

2 Heat half the oil in a large wok over high heat. Stir-fry the chicken and prawns in batches for 2 minutes or until golden. Remove from the wok and set aside.

3 Return the wok to high heat, add the remaining oil, the onion, and the carrot and stir-fry for 2 minutes or until golden. Add the garlic and ginger and stir-fry for 30 seconds or until fragrant. Add the cauliflower and stir-fry for 2–3 minutes or until tender. Add the snow peas and peas and stir-fry for a further 1–2 minutes or until just tender.

4 Return the chicken and prawns to the wok. Add the tamari and chili sauce and stir-fry until heated through. Remove from the heat and stir in the cilantro. Serve with hot chili sauce and lime halves.

vegan

This delicious salad is ready in minutes and can be served as a side dish, or with some grilled chicken or lamb for a more substantial main course.

Pea, avocado, walnut, and herb couscous

Preparation time: 10 minutes
Cooking time: 5 minutes
Serves 4

1 cup shelled fresh or frozen green peas

5½ oz sugarsnap peas, trimmed and sliced

1 cup couscous

¼ cup walnut halves, lightly toasted and coarsely chopped

½ firm ripe avocado, peeled, stone removed, diced

2 tablespoons coarsely chopped flat-leaf (Italian) parsley leaves

2 tablespoons coarsely chopped mint leaves

1 tablespoon snipped chives

1 tablespoon lemon juice

1 tablespoon olive oil

1 Cook the green peas in a saucepan of boiling water for 3–4 minutes or until just tender, adding the sugarsnap peas for the last 2 minutes of cooking time. Refresh under cold running water. Drain and set aside.

2 Put the couscous in a large heatproof bowl. Pour over 1 cup boiling water. Cover and set aside to steam for 3 minutes. Fluff and separate grains with a fork.

3 Add the peas, walnuts, avocado, herbs, lemon juice, and olive oil to the couscous. Season to taste with sea salt and freshly ground black pepper and gently stir to combine.

tip Squeeze a little lemon juice over the avocado to prevent it from browning.

gluten-free (see tips)

These peas are delicious served with roast chicken.
You can replace the butter with olive oil, but the
flavor won't be quite as good.

Petit pois

Preparation time: 10 minutes
Cooking time: 10 minutes
Serves 4

1 tablespoon butter
1–2 slices bacon, cut into thin strips
4 scallions, trimmed and sliced
1 garlic clove, crushed
2 cups shelled fresh or frozen
green peas
½ cup low-sodium chicken stock
1 baby romaine lettuce,
trimmed and shredded
Pinch of granulated sugar

1 Melt the butter in a large non-stick frying pan over medium–high heat. Add the bacon and scallions and cook, stirring, for 2–3 minutes, or until light golden. Add the garlic and cook, stirring, for 30 seconds.

2 Add the peas and stock, cover and simmer for 3–4 minutes or until the peas are bright green and tender-crisp. Add the lettuce and sugar and cook, stirring, until the lettuce has just wilted. Serve immediately.

tips For a gluten-free version, use gluten-free bacon and stock.

Fresh peas may require an extra 1–2 minutes of cooking time to become tender.

Pea and paneer curry

(see recipe page 102)

Pea and coconut sundal

(see recipe page 103)

Peas are a rich source of dietary fiber, vitamin C, and vitamin K, as well as a good source of folate, which is essential during pregnancy.

Pea and paneer curry

Preparation time: 15 minutes
Cooking time: 25 minutes
Serves 4

1½ tablespoons peanut oil

7 oz paneer, cut into ⅝-inch cubes (see tip)

1 large red onion, finely chopped

2 garlic cloves, crushed

2 teaspoons finely grated ginger

2 teaspoons brown mustard seeds

1 teaspoon ground cumin

1 teaspoon ground coriander

1 teaspoon garam masala

14-oz can crushed tomatoes

1½ cups fresh or frozen green peas

2 teaspoons lime juice

½ teaspoon brown sugar

Cilantro leaves, to garnish

Steamed basmati rice, to serve

1 Heat 2 teaspoons of the oil in a large non-stick frying pan or wok over medium–high heat. Add half the paneer and stir-fry for 1–2 minutes or until golden brown. Remove from the pan and set aside. Repeat with another 2 teaspoons of the oil and the remaining paneer.

2 Return the pan to medium heat. Add the remaining 2 teaspoons of oil and the onion and cook, stirring, for 2–3 minutes or until golden. Add the garlic, ginger, and spices and cook, stirring, for 1–2 minutes or until fragrant. Add the tomatoes and 1 cup water, bring to the boil, reduce the heat to low, and simmer for 10 minutes.

3 Return the paneer to the pan and add the peas. Simmer for 4–5 minutes or until the peas are tender. Remove from the heat, stir in the lime juice and brown sugar, and serve garnished with cilantro, with steamed basmati rice.

tip Paneer is a firm Indian cottage cheese that holds its shape during cooking. You could substitute baked ricotta.

« pictured pages 100–101

vegan • gluten-free

A sundal is an Indian side dish made from dried legumes, spices, and coconut. Try serving it alongside your favorite curry with some flat bread and a dollop of natural yogurt.

Pea and coconut sundal

Preparation time: 15 minutes
(plus overnight soaking)
Cooking time: 55 minutes
Serves 4–6

1 cup dried green split peas, soaked in cold water overnight, drained

1 tablespoon peanut oil

1 large red onion, thinly sliced

1 long red chili, seeded and finely chopped

2 garlic cloves, thinly sliced

1 teaspoon brown mustard seeds

1 teaspoon ground cumin

½ teaspoon garam masala

¼ cup unsweetened shredded coconut, lightly toasted

1 tablespoon lime juice

1 Put the split peas in a large saucepan. Cover with cold water and bring to the boil. Reduce the heat to low and simmer for 30–45 minutes or until tender. Drain and set aside.

2 Heat the oil in a large wok or non-stick frying pan over medium heat. Add the onion and cook, stirring, for 3 minutes or until golden. Add the chili, garlic, and spices and cook, stirring, for 1 minute or until fragrant.

3 Add the cooked peas and ½ cup water and cook, stirring, for 5 minutes or until the water has evaporated and the sundal is heated through. Stir in the coconut and lime juice and serve.

« pictured page 101

Snow peas, like all peas, are one of the best vegetable sources of dietary fiber. They are also packed with vitamin C, vitamin B$_3$ (niacin), folate, and potassium.

Honey-glazed pork with snow pea, cabbage, and sprout slaw

Preparation time: 15 minutes
Cooking time: 20 minutes
Serves 4

¼ cup orange juice

2 tablespoons honey

2 tablespoons mirin

1½ tablespoons low-sodium tamari

1 teaspoon finely grated ginger

1 teaspoon olive oil

1 lb 2 oz pork fillets

7 oz snow peas, trimmed and thinly sliced

¼ small red cabbage (about 14 oz), trimmed and shredded

1 cup pea sprouts, trimmed

2 teaspoons lightly toasted sesame seeds

1 teaspoon sesame oil

Thinly sliced scallions, to garnish

1 Preheat the oven to 400°F. Combine the orange juice, honey, mirin, 1 tablespoon tamari, and the ginger in a small saucepan. Simmer over medium heat for 3–4 minutes or until syrupy and reduced by half. Set aside.

2 Place a wire rack over a baking tray lined with parchment paper. Heat the oil in a large non-stick frying pan over high heat. Cook the pork for 1–2 minutes each side or until browned. Transfer the pork to the prepared rack and brush with half the reserved glaze. Roast for 10 minutes for medium, or until cooked to your liking. Remove, cover loosely with foil, and set aside to rest for 3 minutes.

3 Place the snow peas, cabbage, pea sprouts, sesame seeds, remaining 2 teaspoons tamari, and sesame oil in a large bowl and toss to combine.

4 To serve, thickly slice the pork. Divide the salad and pork between serving plates, drizzle the pork with a little of the remaining glaze, and garnish with the scallions.

tips For a gluten-free version, use gluten-free tamari.

It is essential to line the baking tray with parchment paper, to prevent the glaze from burning on the bottom of the tray.

borlotti beans, fava beans, & green beans

borlotti beans, fava beans, & green beans

Borlotti beans, fava beans, and green beans (as well as Chinese long beans) all grow on climbing plants or rounded bushes and consist of long narrow pods filled with kidney-shaped seeds. Some seeds are eaten fresh, either with or without their pods, while others are more often removed from their pods before being dried and stored. All beans are highly nutritious – they're good sources of dietary fiber, vitamin C, and folate.

borlotti beans

BORLOTTI BEANS, ALSO known as cranberry beans or Roman beans, are creamy white beans with red markings on the pods and the seeds. They are another variety of the same species as dwarf or bush green beans, *Phaseolus vulgaris*, and can be eaten either immature and fresh, or mature and dried. During cooking, the seeds lose their bright markings and turn a light brown color. The cooked dried beans have a creamy, meaty texture and a nutty flavor.

Fresh young borlotti beans are available in spring. The pod is inedible; only the seeds are eaten, and the fresh beans do not require soaking before cooking.

Dried borlotti beans do require soaking, and after cooking they are delicious in soups, stews, or salads. Canned borlotti beans are also available, and they need only to be drained and rinsed.

Borlotti beans are popular in Italian and Portuguese cuisine. Flavor-wise, they're a perfect fit with Mediterranean ingredients such as vine-ripened tomatoes, olive oil, parmesan, and fresh basil.

Like all beans and other legumes, borlotti beans are an excellent source of plant protein, and therefore a wonderful addition to vegetarian diets. They can be used to replace some of the meat content in many recipes, for both added nutrition and reduced overall cost. They are rich in dietary fiber and vitamin C and are a good source of folate, which is essential during pregnancy.

Cooking instructions

Stovetop

To prepare fresh borlotti beans, first remove the seeds from the pods (discard the pods). Cook in a large saucepan of barely simmering water for 30 minutes or until tender. It is important not to boil the water or the beans will become tough. Drain.

To prepare dried borlotti beans, soak 1 cup dried beans in cold water overnight. Rinse and drain. Put them in a large saucepan, add cold water to cover the beans by 2 inches, and bring to the boil. Reduce the heat to low and simmer for 45 minutes–1 hour or until tender. Drain.

Pressure cooker

Soak 1 cup dried beans in a large bowl of cold water overnight. Rinse and drain. Put them in a pressure cooker with 4 cups water. Cook at high pressure for 10–15 minutes.

If using unsoaked dried borlotti beans, cook at high pressure for 30–35 minutes.

NUTRITION	PER 100 G (3½ OZ) COOKED DRIED BORLOTTI BEANS
Energy	135 cal
Protein	9.3 g
Fat	0.5 g
Saturated fat	0.1 g
Carbohydrate	14.5 g
Dietary fiber	10 g
Folate	207 µg
Magnesium	50 mg
Phosphorus	135 mg

fava beans

FAVA BEANS, *VICIA FABA*, also known as broad or faba beans, have large, flattened, light green pods containing flat kidney-shaped beans. Along with lentils, peas, and chickpeas, fava beans are believed to have been part of eastern Mediterranean diets from around 6000 BC.

Fava beans are a hardy crop, able to withstand harsh and cold climates. Environmentally beneficial, they are often used as a winter rotation crop to prevent soil erosion and improve soil health by fixing nitrogen in the soil.

Fava beans can be eaten at three different stages of maturity. While still young, they can be steamed and served whole (pods and all), just like green beans. The young leaves can also be eaten raw or cooked like spinach.

When they're mature, the beans need to be removed from the pods. Inside the pods, the individual beans are covered in a thin, gray, papery skin. In just-mature beans this skin is tender and fine to eat, but in more mature beans the inner skin tends to be tough and needs to be removed. To remove the inner skins, cook the beans in boiling water for 1–2 minutes, drain, refresh in cold water, then gently squeeze the bright green bean from the skin. This is known as double shelling.

Finally, fava beans can be left to grow until they're fully mature and the seeds have dried. The beans are then soaked and cooked.

Fava beans are also available frozen; in this state they are sold shelled. Frozen fava beans are a handy option because the fresh ones have only a short season in early spring.

Canned fava beans are mature fava beans that have been double-shelled, dried, and cooked. Simply drain and rinse them and they're ready for use.

Fava beans can be dried and ground to make flour, or fried and then salted to produce a crunchy snack. Fresh or dried, they can be added to salads, soups, and hearty casseroles.

Fava beans are an excellent source of plant protein, as well as rich in dietary fiber and slow-release carbohydrates, making them an excellent choice for people with diabetes. They are high in vitamin A, which is essential for good eye health, and the B vitamins, important for energy production. They are a good source of the minerals iron and manganese.

Cooking instructions

Stovetop

To cook fresh mature fava beans, remove the seeds from the pods (discard the pods). Cook in a large saucepan of boiling water for 2–3 minutes or until just tender. Drain and refresh in cold water. Peel off the outer skins and discard.

To cook dried fava beans, soak 1 cup dried beans in a large bowl of cold water overnight. Drain and rinse. Place in a large saucepan, add cold water to cover the beans by 2 inches, and bring to the boil. Reduce the heat to low and simmer for 1–1½ hours or until tender. Drain.

Pressure cooker

To cook dried fava beans, soak 1 cup dried beans in a large bowl of cold water overnight. Drain and rinse. Place in a pressure cooker with 4 cups water. Cook at high pressure for 10–15 minutes or until tender.

If using unsoaked dried fava beans, cook at high pressure for 25–30 minutes.

NUTRITION	PER 100 G (3½ OZ) COOKED FRESH SHELLED FAVA BEANS
Energy	60 cal
Protein	7.4 g
Fat	0.5 g
Saturated fat	0.1 g
Carbohydrate	2.4 g
Dietary fiber	7.6 g
Potassium	202 mg
Iron	1.7 mg

green beans

GREEN BEANS, ALSO KNOWN as string beans, snap beans, and French beans, are typically eaten fresh, not dried. And in fact they're not always green, but may be yellow, gray-green, or even purple. The types most commonly sold in supermarkets and greengrocers are dwarf or bush beans, varieties of *Phaseolus vulgaris*. They're picked when the pods are immature, 4–8 inches in length, and contain small, soft, pale green seeds that are just starting to form. The pod and seeds are eaten as a whole.

Green beans require minimal preparation – just snap or cut off the ends and cook them whole or sliced. Most supermarket beans are "stringless" but some varieties have a "string" along their length that needs to be removed before slicing or cooking. They're best lightly steamed or boiled to retain their nutrients, color, and flavor.

Raw fresh beans should snap when broken – avoid limp beans and mature beans with a tough skin.

Green beans are extremely versatile and can be eaten raw in salads or as a snack, added to stir-fries, soups, curries, and stews, or steamed and served as a side dish. They are delicious simply steamed, drizzled with olive oil and sprinkled with toasted nuts such as almonds, walnuts, or pine nuts. They are also delicious topped with shaved parmesan or crumbled feta with some freshly grated lemon zest.

Green beans are in season from late spring to early autumn (fall), so their quality and value are best at this time, although they're available year-round. They're high in protein, and a rich source of the vitamins K, C, folate, and B_2, and vitamin A in the form of carotenoids. They are also a good source of the minerals manganese and iron. Green beans have a low GI and a low calorie count.

Cooking instructions

Place beans in a steamer over a saucepan of boiling water, cover, and steam for 2 minutes or until just tender. Alternatively, cook them in a saucepan of boiling water for 2 minutes or until just tender. Drain.

NUTRITION	PER 100 G (3½ OZ) COOKED GREEN BEANS
Energy	21 cal
Protein	1.5 g
Fat	0.2 g
Saturated fat	0 g
Carbohydrate	2.2 g
Dietary fiber	2.5 g
Folate	33 µg
Iron	1.1 mg

Bruschetta with fava beans, marinated bell peppers, and goat's cheese

(see recipe page 114)

**Fava bean dip with
spiced pita crisps**

(see recipe page 115)

vegetarian • gluten-free (see tips)

Fresh fava beans have a short season in spring, and they can be tricky to find. Frozen ones are a great substitute, and the nutritional difference is negligible thanks to flash-freezing techniques. Frozen beans need to have their tough skins removed, whereas very young fresh fava beans can be eaten in their pods, like green beans.

Bruschetta with fava beans, marinated bell peppers, and goat's cheese

Preparation time: 15 minutes
Cooking time: 10 minutes
(plus 20 minutes steaming)
Serves 4

2 red bell peppers, halved and seeded (see tip)

2 tablespoons coarsely chopped basil, plus extra leaves to garnish

1 tablespoon salted baby capers, rinsed, drained, and chopped

2 teaspoons olive oil

2 teaspoons red wine vinegar

1½ cups shelled fresh or frozen fava beans

2¾ oz (75 g) soft goat's cheese, crumbled

8 slices sourdough bread, toasted

Mint leaves, to garnish

1 Preheat the grill (broiler) to high. Place the bell peppers on a baking tray. Grill until the skin blackens and blisters. Transfer to a large bowl, cover with plastic wrap, and set aside to steam for 20 minutes. Carefully peel off the skin and discard. Cut the bell peppers into ½-inch-wide strips.

2 Put the chopped basil, capers, olive oil, and vinegar in a large bowl. Add the bell peppers and stir to coat. Season to taste with sea salt and freshly ground black pepper.

3 Cook the fava beans in a saucepan of boiling water for 3 minutes or until tender. Refresh under cold running water. Drain. Peel off the skins and discard.

4 Add the beans and goat's cheese to the bell peppers and gently toss to combine. Spoon onto the toasted bread. Serve immediately garnished with basil and mint leaves.

tips For a gluten-free version, use gluten-free bread.

You could use purchased roasted or wood-fired bell peppers; you'll need about 1 cup.

« pictured page 112

This versatile dip can also be served with vegetable sticks, as a topping for bruschetta, or as part of a mezze platter.

Fava bean dip with spiced pita crisps

Preparation time: 15 minutes
Cooking time: 10 minutes
Serves 4–6

2 rounds whole-wheat pita bread

1 teaspoon za'atar, plus extra to garnish

Olive oil spray, for coating

3 cups shelled fresh or frozen fava beans

¼ cup fresh ricotta

1 tablespoon lemon juice

1 tablespoon olive oil, plus extra to garnish

2 tablespoons finely chopped mint

2 tablespoons finely chopped flat-leaf (Italian) parsley

1 Preheat the oven to 400°F. Cut each pita bread into 12 triangles. Place the triangles on two large baking trays, sprinkle with the za'atar, and spray lightly with oil. Bake, turning once, for 7–8 minutes or until golden.

2 Meanwhile, cook the fava beans in a saucepan of boiling water for 3 minutes or until just tender, refresh them under cold running water, and drain well. Peel off the skins and discard.

3 Put the fava beans, ricotta, lemon juice, and olive oil in a blender or food processor and process to a rough paste. Season to taste with sea salt and freshly ground black pepper. Add the mint and parsley and pulse for a few seconds or until just combined.

4 Serve the dip with the pita crisps, garnished with a drizzle of olive oil and a little extra za'atar.

tips For a gluten-free version, use gluten-free pita bread.

The dip will keep, stored in an airtight container in the refrigerator, for up to 3 days.

« **pictured page 113**

dairy-free • gluten-free

Poaching is a wonderful way to cook chicken breast. It's fat-free and keeps the chicken deliciously moist and tender.

Poached chicken, fava bean, and apple salad with toasted seeds

Preparation time: 20 minutes
Cooking time: 40 minutes
Serves 4

1 onion, halved

1 tablespoon black peppercorns

4 x 4½-oz chicken breasts

2⅓ cups shelled fresh or frozen fava beans

2¼ cups firmly packed baby arugula or spinach leaves

1 red apple, cored and diced

2 tablespoons lightly toasted sunflower seeds

2 tablespoons lightly toasted pepitas (pumpkin seeds)

2 tablespoons raw almonds, coarsely chopped

2 tablespoons coarsely chopped mint

1 tablespoon coarsely chopped dill

1 tablespoon olive oil

1 tablespoon white balsamic vinegar

2 tablespoons apple juice

1 Put the onion, peppercorns, and a pinch of sea salt in a large saucepan with 5 cups cold water and bring to the boil. Add the chicken breasts, reduce the heat to low, and simmer gently for 5 minutes. Remove from the heat, cover, and set aside to continue poaching for 30 minutes. Remove the chicken from the poaching liquid (discard the liquid) and set aside to cool. Coarsely chop the chicken.

2 Meanwhile, cook the fava beans in a large saucepan of boiling water for 3 minutes. Refresh under cold running water. Drain. Peel off the skins and discard.

3 Put the chicken, fava beans, arugula leaves, apple, seeds, almonds, and herbs in a large bowl. Whisk together the olive oil, vinegar, and apple juice. Add to the salad and gently toss to combine. Serve immediately.

tip To prevent the apple from discoloring, squeeze a little lemon juice over it.

vegetarian • dairy-free • gluten-free

Borlotti beans have a creamy rich texture and nutty flavor that is a perfect match with the honey-roasted squash and hazelnuts. They are also nutritious, being high in protein and fiber.

Honey-roasted squash, borlotti bean, broccolini, and hazelnut salad

Preparation time: 15 minutes
Cooking time: 40 minutes
Serves 4

1½ tablespoons honey

1½ tablespoons olive oil

2 teaspoons coarsely chopped rosemary

1 lb 12 oz winter squash (approximately 1 small squash), seeded and cut into wedges (see tips)

2 teaspoons red wine vinegar

2 bunches broccolini, trimmed

14 oz-can borlotti beans, drained and rinsed (see tips)

1 head radicchio, trimmed and leaves torn

2 tablespoons lightly toasted hazelnuts, coarsely chopped

1 Preheat the oven to 400°F. Line a large baking tray with parchment paper. Combine 1 tablespoon honey, 1 tablespoon olive oil, and the rosemary in a large bowl. Add the squash and toss to coat. Place on the prepared tray and roast for 30–40 minutes or until golden, turning halfway through the cooking time.

2 Meanwhile, combine the remaining honey and oil and the vinegar in a small bowl. Set aside.

3 Cook the broccolini in a saucepan of boiling water until just tender. Drain. Combine the squash, broccolini, borlotti beans, radicchio, and hazelnuts in a large bowl. Add the honey dressing and gently toss to combine. Season to taste with sea salt and freshly ground black pepper.

tips Butternut squash works well in this salad.

You can replace the canned borlotti beans with 1½ cups cooked borlotti beans.

vegetarian • gluten-free (see tips)

This risotto uses a mix of rice and quinoa to make it more nutritious. Quinoa is a good source of protein and is rich in dietary fiber, which is linked to a reduced risk of cardiovascular disease, cancer, and type 2 diabetes. It is also high in manganese, and a good source of phosphorus, magnesium, and folate.

Quinoa risotto with beans, lemon, and parmesan

Preparation time: 15 minutes
Cooking time: 35 minutes
Serves 4

2 cups shelled fresh or frozen fava beans

4 cups low-sodium vegetable or chicken stock

1 tablespoon olive oil

1 leek, white part only, thinly sliced

2 garlic cloves, crushed

2 teaspoons thyme leaves

¾ cup arborio rice

½ cup white quinoa, rinsed and drained

⅓ cup white wine

1 cup shelled fresh or frozen green peas

¼ cup finely grated parmesan cheese, plus extra to serve

1 teaspoon finely grated lemon zest

Mint leaves, to garnish

1 Cook the fava beans in a saucepan of boiling water for 1 minute. Refresh under cold running water. Drain. Peel off the skins and discard. Set aside.

2 Put the stock in a large saucepan and bring to the boil over high heat. Reduce the heat to low and keep the stock at a simmer.

3 Heat the oil in a large heavy-based saucepan over medium heat. Add the leek and cook, stirring, for 5 minutes or until soft. Add the garlic and thyme leaves and cook, stirring, for 1 minute or until fragrant. Add the rice and white quinoa and stir for 1–2 minutes or until the grains are well coated in the oil. Add the wine and simmer until reduced by half.

4 Gradually add the simmering stock, a cup at a time, stirring constantly and making sure the stock is absorbed before you add more. This will take 15–20 minutes; the rice should be al dente yet creamy.

5 Stir in the peas and fava beans. Simmer for 2–3 minutes or until the vegetables are just tender, then remove from the heat and stir in the parmesan and lemon zest. Cover and set aside for 3 minutes. Season to taste with sea salt and freshly ground black pepper. Serve garnished with mint, with extra parmesan.

tip For a gluten-free version, use gluten-free stock.

This stew is full of flavor. The combination of chickpeas and bulgur provides a complete protein, ideal for vegetarians.

Vegetable and harissa stew with pistachio and herb bulgur

Preparation time: 20 minutes
Cooking time: 30 minutes
Serves 4

2 cups shelled fresh or frozen fava beans
1 tablespoon olive oil
1 large onion, diced
3 garlic cloves, thinly sliced
1 teaspoon finely grated ginger
1 teaspoon ground cumin
1/2 teaspoon ground turmeric
14 oz-can diced tomatoes
1 cup vegetable stock
1 teaspoon harissa paste, or to taste, plus extra to serve
2 carrots, peeled and coarsely chopped
14 oz-can chickpeas, drained and rinsed
1 red bell pepper, seeded and coarsely chopped
5 1/2 oz green beans, sliced
Cilantro leaves, to garnish

PISTACHIO AND HERB BULGUR
2/3 cup coarse bulgur
2 tablespoons shelled unsalted pistachios, coarsely chopped
2 tablespoons raisins
2 tablespoons each coarsely chopped flat-leaf (Italian) parsley and cilantro

1 Cook the fava beans in a saucepan of boiling water for 1 minute. Refresh under cold running water. Drain. Peel off the skins and discard. Set aside.

2 Heat the oil in a large saucepan over medium heat. Add the onion and cook, stirring, for 5 minutes or until softened, then add the garlic, ginger, cumin, and turmeric and cook, stirring, for 1 minute, or until fragrant. Add the tomatoes, stock, and harissa paste and bring to the boil.

3 Add the chopped carrot and simmer for 10 minutes. Add the chickpeas and bell pepper and simmer for a further 5 minutes. Add the fava beans and green beans and simmer for 5 minutes or until the beans are tender.

4 Meanwhile, put the bulgur in a large heatproof bowl. Add 2 cups boiling water and set aside to soak for 5 minutes. Drain and squeeze out any excess moisture by pressing with the back of a spoon. Return the bulgur to the bowl and add the pistachios, raisins, and herbs. Season to taste with sea salt and freshly ground black pepper.

5 Serve the vegetable stew on the bulgur, garnished with cilantro leaves and a dollop of harissa.

tips Harissa, a fiery Tunisian chili paste, adds a kick to this vegetable stew. You can substitute another type of chili paste, such as sambal oelek.

You can use fine instead of coarse bulgur. It will need less soaking, just 2–3 minutes.

vegan

Fresh green beans and lima beans require little cooking and are delicious served slightly al dente. A rich source of dietary fiber, vitamin K, manganese, vitamin C, and carotenoids (a precursor to vitamin A), they also have a low GI and are low in calories.

Green beans with walnuts and lemon

Preparation time: 15 minutes
Cooking time: 5 minutes
Serves 4

5½ oz green beans, trimmed

5½ oz lima beans, trimmed

2 teaspoons thinly sliced lemon zest

2 teaspoons lemon juice

2 teaspoons olive oil

¼ cup lightly toasted walnut halves, coarsely chopped

1 Cook the green beans and lima beans in a saucepan of boiling water for 2 minutes or until just tender. Add the lemon zest for the last 30 seconds of cooking time. Drain and transfer to a serving platter.

2 Combine the lemon juice and olive oil. Drizzle the dressing over the beans and top with the walnuts. Serve immediately.

tips Drizzle the beans with the dressing just before serving; otherwise the lemon juice will start to discolor the beans.

This salad is delicious served warm or at room temperature.

Ginger beef and bean stir-fry

(see recipe page 126)

Chinese long beans or yard-long beans are dark green and crunchy.
If you can't find them, substitute regular green beans.

Ginger beef and bean stir-fry

Preparation time: 15 minutes
Cooking time: 15 minutes
Serves 4

2½ cups fresh or frozen edamame (soy beans)

1 tablespoon peanut or macadamia oil

1 lb 2 oz lean rump steak, thinly sliced across the grain

1 white onion, thinly sliced

1¼-inch piece ginger, peeled and cut into thin matchsticks

1 long red chili, seeded and finely chopped

7 oz Chinese long beans, trimmed and sliced

1 red bell pepper, seeded and thinly sliced

2 tablespoons oyster sauce

1 tablespoon low-sodium soy sauce

1 tablespoon Chinese rice wine

Steamed brown rice, to serve (optional)

Scallions, thinly sliced, to garnish (optional)

1 Cook the edamame in a saucepan of boiling water for 1 minute. Refresh under cold running water. Drain. Remove the beans from the pods (discard pods) and set aside.

2 Heat half the oil in a large wok over high heat. Stir-fry the beef in two batches for 2 minutes or until golden. Remove from the wok and set aside.

3 Return the wok to high heat. Add the remaining oil and the onion and stir-fry for 2 minutes. Add the ginger and chili and stir-fry for 30 seconds or until fragrant. Add the Chinese long beans, bell pepper and 2 tablespoons water and stir-fry for 2 minutes or until the vegetables are almost tender-crisp.

4 Return the beef to the wok with the reserved edamame and the oyster sauce, soy sauce, and rice wine and stir-fry for 1–2 minutes or until heated through. Serve immediately on steamed brown rice, if desired, garnished with scallions.

« pictured pages 124–125

Pasta e fagioli is a hearty rustic Italian soup of "pasta and beans." Every region of Italy has its own version of the recipe, but most use dried borlotti or cannellini beans. Dried borlotti beans are off-white in color, with red markings. During cooking they turn light brown.

Pasta e fagioli

Preparation time: 15 minutes
(plus overnight soaking)
Cooking time: 1½ hours
Serves 4

¾ cup dried borlotti beans, soaked in cold water overnight

1 tablespoon olive oil

1 large onion, finely chopped

2 stalks celery, diced

2 slices bacon, trimmed and diced

2 garlic cloves, crushed

2 teaspoons finely chopped rosemary

¼ teaspoon dried chili flakes

1 tablespoon unsalted tomato paste (concentrated purée)

4 cups low-sodium chicken or vegetable stock

14-oz can diced tomatoes

1 cup dried short pasta, such as macaroni

Thinly sliced basil leaves, to garnish

Finely grated parmesan cheese, to serve

1 Put the borlotti beans in a large saucepan, cover with cold water, bring to the boil, then reduce the heat to low and simmer for 45 minutes–1 hour or until tender. Drain and set aside.

2 Heat the olive oil in a large saucepan over medium heat. Add the onion, celery, and bacon and cook, stirring, for 6–7 minutes or until softened. Add the garlic, rosemary, and chili and cook, stirring, for 30 seconds or until fragrant.

3 Add the tomato paste and cook, stirring, for 1 minute, then add the stock, tomatoes, and cooked beans. Bring to the boil, reduce the heat to low, and simmer for 10 minutes. Add the pasta and simmer for 10 minutes or until the pasta is al dente.

4 Season to taste with sea salt and freshly ground black pepper. Serve topped with basil and grated parmesan.

tips For a gluten-free version, use gluten-free bacon, stock, and pasta.

The cooking time of the borlotti beans will vary depending on the age of the beans.

This soup is suitable to freeze. Put it in airtight containers, cool completely, cover, and freeze for up to 2 months.

This pasta is fresh in flavor, and beautifully light — perfect for summer. It's important to use good quality olive oil and ripe tomatoes.

Pasta with beans, prosciutto, tomato, and parmesan

Preparation time: 15 minutes
Cooking time: 15 minutes
Serves 4

2 cups shelled fresh or frozen fava beans

9 oz wholegrain spaghetti, such as wholegrain spelt spaghetti

7 oz green beans, trimmed and sliced

1½ tablespoons extra-virgin olive oil

1 red onion, finely chopped

3½ oz prosciutto, cut into thin strips

3 garlic cloves, thinly sliced

4 roma (plum) tomatoes, seeded and diced

1 tablespoon lemon juice

2 tablespoons coarsely chopped basil

Freshly shaved parmesan cheese, to serve

1 Cook the fava beans in a saucepan of boiling water for 3 minutes or until tender. Refresh under cold running water. Drain. Peel off the skins and discard. Set aside.

2 Cook the spaghetti in a large saucepan of lightly salted boiling water according to the package instructions or until al dente, adding the green beans for the last 2 minutes of cooking time. Drain and set aside with the fava beans.

3 Meanwhile, heat 2 teaspoons of the oil in a large non-stick frying pan over medium heat. Add the onion and cook, stirring, for 5 minutes or until soft. Add the prosciutto and garlic and cook, stirring, for 3 minutes or until the prosciutto is golden. Add the tomatoes and lemon juice and remove from the heat.

4 Add the tomato mixture to the hot pasta with the basil and remaining olive oil. Season to taste with sea salt and freshly ground black pepper and toss to combine. Serve with shaved parmesan.

tips For a gluten-free version, use gluten-free spaghetti and prosciutto.

For a vegetarian version, omit the prosciutto.

You can replace the roma tomatoes with 1½ cups cherry tomatoes, quartered.

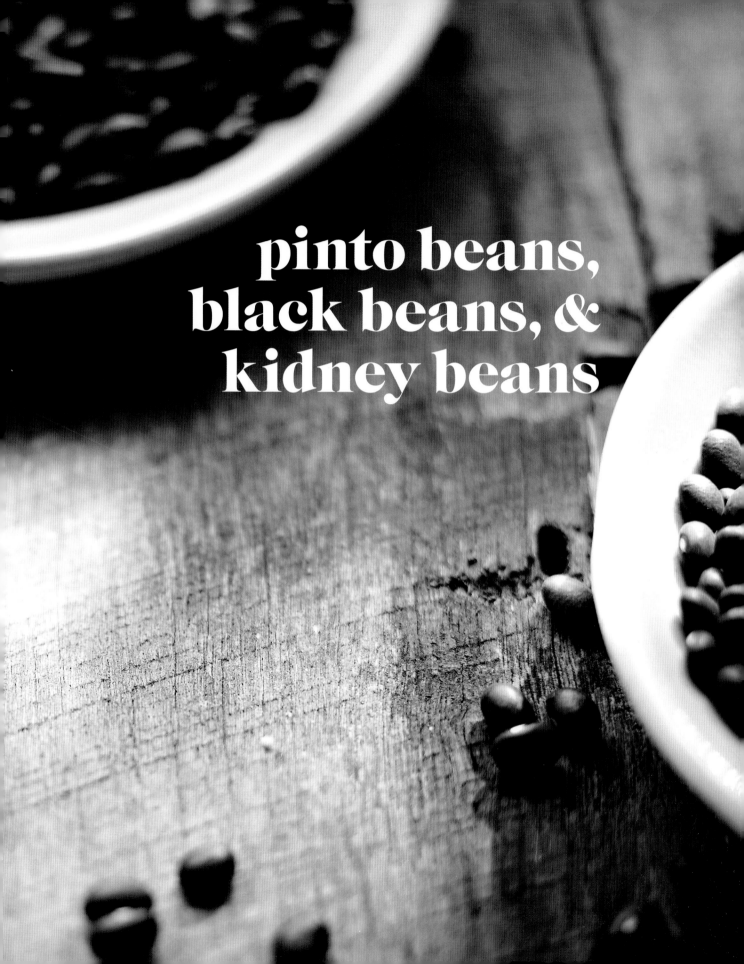

pinto beans, black beans, & kidney beans

pinto beans, black beans, & kidney beans

Pinto beans, black beans, and kidney beans are all varieties of the common garden bean, *Phaseolus vulgaris*, and are widely used in Latin American cooking. They have similar nutritional values and cooking uses and are interchangeable in most recipes. They are sold dried and canned — both forms have similar nutritional values and health benefits.

pinto beans

Pinto beans are very popular in the United States, Mexico, and Brazil. It's been estimated that around 45% of all dried beans consumed in the US are pinto beans.

These small oval beans are tan-brown in color, with distinct reddish-brown splotches on their skin which are usually lost in cooking.

They are eaten whole in soup, as a filling for burritos, and as refried beans, where they are cooked, mashed, then fried. The young fresh pods may also be cooked and eaten as green pinto beans. Cheese, chilies, garlic, onions, spices, tomatoes, cured meats, and rice all make perfect flavor partners.

Pinto beans teamed with rice, polenta, or sweet potatoes are staple dishes throughout South America, especially where meat is scarce. Pinto beans are high in protein (15 g per cup of cooked beans), and when combined with rice or other grains, they form a complete protein, providing a nutritious and inexpensive alternative to meat.

Even aside from their protein content, pinto beans are one of the most nutritious legumes. Packed with dietary fiber, they have a low GI, which stabilizes blood sugar levels and provides heart health benefits. They are rich in folate, magnesium, and potassium, which can also assist healthy heart function.

Cooking instructions

Stovetop
Soak 1 cup dried pinto beans in cold water overnight. Drain, then rinse. Put them in a large saucepan, add cold water to cover the beans by 2 inches, and bring to the boil. Reduce the heat to low and simmer for 1 hour or until tender. Drain.

Pressure cooker
Soak 1 cup dried pinto beans in cold water overnight. Drain, then rinse. Put them in a pressure cooker with 4 cups water. Cook at high pressure for 10–15 minutes or until tender.

If using unsoaked pinto beans, cook at high pressure for 20–30 minutes.

NUTRITION	PER 100 G (3½ OZ) COOKED PINTO BEANS
Energy	142 cal
Protein	9 g
Fat	0.6 g
Saturated fat	0.1 g
Carbohydrate	17 g
Dietary fiber	9 g
Folate	172 µg
Iron	2 mg
Magnesium	50 mg
Potassium	436 mg

black beans

Black beans, also known as black turtle beans, are used extensively in South American, Cajun, and Creole cuisines and are a key ingredient in Mexican and Tex-Mex dishes such as burritos, black bean soup, quesadillas, and tacos. Black beans and rice is a staple dish throughout South America, a simple yet delicious meal that, as well as being highly nutritious, forms a complete protein. That is, rice and black beans together contain all the essential amino acids. The beans also form the basis of the classic Brazilian stew feijoada.

Black beans are distinguished from other beans by their small size, black shiny color, and deep, rich flavor. Their "meaty" flavor and dense creamy texture make them an excellent low-fat, high-protein meat substitute. Even the cooking water is quite flavorful and can be used as stock for making soups or stews. Black beans are popular in many vegetarian recipes as well as being a healthy addition to other soups, salads, dips, and pasta dishes.

Flavor-wise, black beans marry well with chilies, lime, cilantro, mint, tomatoes, garlic, green beans, pork, and seafood.

Nutritionally, like all members of the legume family, black beans contain the winning combination of high protein and high fiber content. Just half a cup of cooked black beans contains more than 8 g dietary fiber. Associated health benefits include regulated blood sugar levels, improved digestive health, reduced risk of colon cancer, and reduced blood cholesterol levels.

The distinctive black outer coating of black beans is rich in phytonutrients, in particular anthocyanin pigments, which are also found in blueberries. These powerful antioxidants may help prevent cancer and heart disease. Black beans are also good sources of folate, magnesium, potassium, and iron.

Cooking instructions

Stovetop

Soak 1 cup dried black beans in a large bowl of cold water overnight. Rinse well, then drain. Put them in a large saucepan, add cold water to cover the beans by 2 inches, and bring to the boil. Reduce the heat to low and simmer for 45 minutes–1 hour or until tender. Drain.

Pressure cooker

Soak 1 cup dried black beans in a large bowl of cold water overnight. Rinse well, then drain. Put them in a pressure cooker with 4 cups water. Cook at high pressure for 5–10 minutes or until tender.

If using unsoaked black beans, cook at high pressure for 10–20 minutes.

NUTRITION	PER 100 G (3½ OZ) COOKED BLACK BEANS
Energy	110 cal
Protein	8.2 g
Fat	0.7 g
Saturated fat	0.1 g
Carbohydrate	12.6 g
Dietary fiber	8.8 g
Folate	140 µg
Iron	2.1 mg
Magnesium	49 mg

kidney beans

Kidney beans are an integral part of the cuisines of Latin America, India, and Pakistan. They are dark red in color and derive their name from their distinctive kidney shape.

They retain their shape and texture during cooking, so they're popular in slow-cooked dishes and curries. They have a mild nutty flavor and a creamy texture, and they absorb the flavors of the liquid, herbs, spices, and other ingredients with which they are cooked.

They work beautifully with flavor partners such as tomatoes, cheese, fresh chili, and corn, and they form the basis of classic dishes such as chili con carne and Creole red beans and rice. They can be used in salads, curries, and stews, or even mashed with olive oil and spices to make a delicious dip to serve with corn chips or vegetable sticks. Try substituting kidney beans for some of the meat in your favorite taco or burrito recipe.

In addition to their impressive high protein and fiber content, kidney beans are a very good source of folate and manganese (essential for energy production). They also provide a vegetarian source of iron, have a low GI, and contain good quantities of magnesium and potassium.

Uncooked kidney beans contain the compound phytohaemagglutinin, which can cause digestive upsets. This compound is deactivated by soaking, rinsing, and then boiling the beans for 10 minutes.

Slow-cookers do not reach high enough temperatures to deactivate the phytohaemagglutinin, so if you're preparing kidney beans in a slow-cooker, you should first soak and boil them as outlined above.

Canned kidney beans are safe to use immediately.

Cooking instructions

Stovetop

Soak 1 cup dried red kidney beans in a large bowl of cold water overnight. Drain, then rinse. Put them in a large saucepan, add cold water to cover the beans by 2 inches, and bring to the boil. Reduce the heat to low and simmer for 45 minutes–1 hour or until tender. Drain.

Pressure cooker

Soak 1 cup dried kidney beans in a large bowl of cold water overnight. Drain, then rinse. Put them in a pressure cooker with 4 cups water. Cook at high pressure for 10–15 minutes or until tender. Drain.

If using unsoaked kidney beans, cook at high pressure for 20–25 minutes or until tender.

NUTRITION	PER 100 G (3½ OZ) COOKED KIDNEY BEANS
Energy	91 cal
Protein	7.9 g
Fat	0.5 g
Saturated fat	0.1 g
Carbohydrate	9.1 g
Dietary fiber	7.2 g
Folate	130 µg
Iron	1.7 mg
Magnesium	38 mg
Potassium	290 mg

These quesadillas form a balanced meal for vegetarians, combining mushrooms (rich in B vitamins, especially niacin, important in energy production) and black beans (low in fat and high in protein). They're delicious for breakfast or lunch.

Breakfast quesadillas with black beans, spinach, and mushrooms

Preparation time: 10 minutes
Cooking time: 10 minutes
Serves 4

1 tablespoon olive oil

2 cups sliced button mushrooms

1 garlic clove, crushed

14-oz can black beans, drained and rinsed (see tips)

1 vine-ripened tomato, diced

4 large wholegrain tortillas

½ cup grated cheddar cheese

1 cup firmly packed baby spinach leaves

Hot chili sauce, to taste

Olive oil spray, for toasting

⅓ cup plain (natural) yogurt

Cilantro leaves, to garnish

1 Heat the olive oil in a large non-stick frying pan over medium–high heat. Add the mushrooms and cook, stirring, for 3–4 minutes or until golden. Add the garlic and cook for 30 seconds or until fragrant. Add the beans and tomato and cook for 1 minute or until heated through. Season to taste with sea salt and freshly ground black pepper. Set aside.

2 Preheat a sandwich press. Spread a quarter of the mushroom mixture over half of a tortilla. Top with a quarter of the cheese, a quarter of the spinach leaves, and chili sauce to taste. Fold the tortilla over to enclose the filling. Repeat with the remaining tortillas and fillings.

3 Spray the quesadillas on both sides with oil. Cook in batches in the sandwich press for 3 minutes or until the quesadillas are crisp and the cheese has melted. Serve with a dollop of yogurt, garnished with cilantro.

tips You can replace the canned beans with 1½ cups cooked black beans.

Instead of using a sandwich press, you can cook the quesadillas in a large non-stick frying pan for 2 minutes each side.

» pictured page 138

vegetarian • gluten-free (see tips)

The addition of beans to the scrambled eggs makes this dish a filling and substantial breakfast, full of protein and dietary fiber to help keep you feeling full until lunchtime.

Scrambled eggs with Mexican beans and spicy tomato salsa

Preparation time: 10 minutes
Cooking time: 10 minutes
Serves 2

4 eggs

2 tablespoons milk

2 teaspoons olive oil

½ small red onion, finely chopped

½ teaspoon sweet paprika

1 garlic clove, crushed

⅔ cup canned or cooked red kidney beans (see tips)

1 cup firmly packed baby spinach leaves

2 slices wholegrain or sourdough toast, to serve

SPICY TOMATO AND CILANTRO SALSA

2 roma (plum) tomatoes, seeded and diced

1 tablespoon finely chopped cilantro, plus extra leaves to garnish

¼ teaspoon dried chili flakes

1 To make the spicy tomato and cilantro salsa, combine all the ingredients in a medium bowl and season to taste with sea salt and freshly ground black pepper. Set aside.

2 Whisk the eggs and milk together in a medium bowl and season to taste with sea salt and freshly ground black pepper. Set aside. Heat the oil in a medium frying pan over medium heat. Add the onion and cook, stirring, for 3–4 minutes or until softened. Add the paprika and garlic and cook, stirring, for 30 seconds. Add the beans and cook, stirring, for 2 minutes or until heated through.

3 Add the spinach and stir until almost wilted. Add the reserved egg mixture, then, using a wooden spoon, push the egg mixture from the edges of the pan to the center. Continue until the eggs are almost set. Season to taste.

4 Serve immediately with toast and spicy tomato and cilantro salsa, garnished with cilantro.

tips For a gluten-free version, use gluten-free bread.

You can replace the red kidney beans with black beans or pinto beans.

» pictured page 139

**Breakfast quesadillas
with black beans,
spinach, and mushrooms**

(see recipe page 136)

Scrambled eggs with Mexican beans and spicy tomato salsa

(see recipe page 137)

vegan • gluten-free (see tips)

The kidney beans give this squash soup body and a delicious thick texture. Red kidney beans, like all legumes, contain various phytochemicals that help to protect against cancer and heart disease and may help to lower cholesterol.

Squash, bean, and coconut soup

Preparation time: 15 minutes
Cooking time: 30 minutes
Serves 4

1 tablespoon olive or coconut oil

1 large onion, coarsely chopped

2 celery stalks, trimmed and diced

2 garlic cloves, crushed

2 teaspoons finely grated ginger

2 teaspoons curry powder

1 small (about 2 lb 4 oz) butternut squash, peeled, seeded, and coarsely chopped

4 cups low-sodium vegetable or chicken stock

14-oz can red kidney beans or pinto beans, drained and rinsed

1/3 cup coconut milk, plus extra to garnish

Lime juice, to taste

Toasted coconut flakes, to garnish

Cilantro leaves, to garnish

1 Heat the olive oil in a large saucepan over medium heat. Add the onion and celery and cook, stirring, for 6–7 minutes or until softened. Add the garlic, ginger, and curry powder and cook, stirring, for 1 minute or until fragrant.

2 Add the squash and stock. Bring to the boil, then reduce the heat to low and simmer, partially covered, for 10 minutes. Add the beans and simmer for 5–10 minutes or until the squash is tender. Set aside to cool slightly.

3 Blend the soup, in batches, in a blender until smooth and creamy. Return the soup to a clean saucepan and stir over medium heat until heated through. Stir in the coconut milk and season to taste with sea salt, freshly ground black pepper, and lime juice.

4 Serve drizzled with extra coconut milk and garnished with toasted coconut flakes and cilantro.

tips For a gluten-free version, use gluten-free stock.

This soup is suitable to freeze. Put it in airtight containers and cool completely. Cover and freeze for up to 2 months.

» pictured page 142

vegetarian

Black beans add flavor and texture to this cornbread, as well as a good
hit of dietary fiber. Pinto beans or red kidney beans would work just as well.
Preheating the frying pan in the oven ensures a crisp golden base.

Black bean, cheese, and chili cornbread

Preparation time: 15 minutes
Cooking time: 30 minutes
Serves 8–10

Olive oil spray, for greasing

1 cup fine polenta (cornmeal)

1 cup all-purpose flour

2 teaspoons baking powder

1 cup buttermilk

2 eggs

¼ cup unsalted butter, melted

1 cup drained canned or cooked black
beans, rinsed

½ cup grated cheddar cheese

2 tablespoons coarsely
chopped cilantro

1 long green chili, seeded and
finely chopped

1 Preheat the oven to 350°F. Lightly spray an 8-inch round
ovenproof frying pan or baking dish with oil.

2 Sift the polenta, flour, baking powder, and a large pinch of salt
into a large bowl. Whisk the buttermilk, eggs, and melted butter
together in a medium bowl. Add the buttermilk mixture to the
flour mixture and stir to combine. Stir in the black beans, cheese,
cilantro, and chili.

3 Place the prepared frying pan or baking dish in the oven to heat
for 5 minutes. Spoon the batter into the heated pan and smooth
the surface with the back of the spoon. Bake for 25–30 minutes or
until the cornbread is golden and a skewer inserted into the center
comes out clean. Set aside to cool for 5 minutes before cutting
into wedges. Serve warm or at room temperature.

tip This cornbread is delicious served with curries or soups,
or just on its own.

» **pictured page 143**

**Squash, bean, and
coconut soup**

(see recipe page 140)

Black bean, cheese, and chili cornbread

(see recipe page 141)

Tacos can be healthy! Spicy marinated prawns and a crisp cabbage and bean salad with a creamy, tangy yogurt-based dressing make these tacos light and fresh.

Prawn tacos with black bean and cabbage salad

Preparation time: 20 minutes
(plus 20 minutes marinating)
Cooking time: 5 minutes
Serves 4

1 tablespoon lime juice

2 teaspoons olive oil

1 garlic clove, crushed

1 teaspoon ground cumin

½ teaspoon dried chili flakes

24 peeled raw prawns (shrimp), deveined, tails intact

8 small corn tortillas, warmed

Lime halves, to garnish

Cilantro leaves, to garnish

BLACK BEAN AND CABBAGE SALAD

¼ green cabbage (about 14 oz), trimmed and shredded

14-oz can black beans, drained and rinsed (see tips)

1 large carrot, peeled and coarsely grated

½ small red onion, thinly sliced

2 tablespoons coarsely chopped cilantro

¼ cup plain (natural) yogurt

2 teaspoons lime juice

1 chipotle pepper in adobo sauce, coarsely chopped (see tips)

1 Combine the lime juice, oil, garlic, cumin, and chili flakes in a shallow glass or ceramic dish. Add the prawns and stir to coat. Cover and set aside in the refrigerator to marinate for 20 minutes.

2 Meanwhile, for the black bean and cabbage salad, combine the cabbage, black beans, carrot, onion, and cilantro in a large bowl. Process the yogurt, lime juice, and chipotle pepper in a food processor or blender until smooth. Add to the salad and gently toss to combine. Set aside.

3 Heat a large grill pan or non-stick frying pan over high heat. Add the prawns and cook for 1 minute each side or until lightly charred and just cooked through. Serve in warm tortillas with the black bean and cabbage salad, garnished with lime and cilantro.

tips You can replace the canned black beans with 1½ cups cooked black beans.

Chipotle peppers in adobo sauce are available from Mexican food stores. You can substitute 1–2 teaspoons of Tabasco chipotle sauce, available from major supermarkets, or another brand of chipotle sauce.

This salad is equally delicious with or without the chicken. Even as a vegetarian dish, it provides a complete protein, thanks to the combination of quinoa and black beans.

Quinoa, black bean, chicken, sweetcorn, and pea salad

Preparation time: 15 minutes
Cooking time: 30 minutes
Serves 4

1 cup quinoa, rinsed and drained (see tips)

1 cup fresh or frozen green peas

2 x 7-oz chicken breasts

1 sweetcorn cob, husk and silk removed

14-oz can black beans, drained and rinsed (see tips)

¼ cup mint leaves, coarsely chopped, plus extra whole leaves to garnish

1½ tablespoons lime juice

1½ tablespoons extra-virgin olive oil

1 teaspoon honey

Pinch of dried chili flakes

1 Put the quinoa in a large saucepan with 1¾ cups cold water. Bring to the boil, reduce the heat to low, cover, and simmer until all the water has been absorbed, about 12–15 minutes. Transfer to a bowl and set aside for 10 minutes.

2 Meanwhile, cook the peas in a saucepan of boiling water until just tender. Refresh under cold running water. Drain well and add to the bowl with the quinoa.

3 Cut each chicken breast horizontally through the middle to give 4 thin fillets. Heat a large grill pan or non-stick frying pan over high heat. Add the corn and cook, turning, for 6–8 minutes or until lightly charred. Remove the corn from the pan and set aside. Add the chicken and cook for 2–3 minutes each side or until golden and cooked through. Set the chicken aside with the corn to cool slightly. Cut the kernels from the corn and thinly slice the chicken. Add the corn, chicken, black beans, and mint to the quinoa mixture.

4 Whisk the lime juice, olive oil, honey, and chili flakes together in a small bowl. Add to the quinoa mixture, season to taste with sea salt and freshly ground black pepper, and gently toss to combine. Garnish with extra mint leaves and serve.

tip You can replace the canned black beans with 1½ cups cooked black beans, or you can use red kidney beans or pinto beans.

Quinoa has a natural coating of saponins, which have a bitter taste. The saponins dissolve easily in water, and most quinoa is sold pre-rinsed to remove the bitterness. It's important, however, to rinse quinoa until the water runs clear to remove any residual bitterness.

vegan • gluten-free

Pinto beans are very popular throughout the US, Mexico, and Brazil, and are traditionally used to make refried beans. If you can't find them, substitute red kidney beans.

Home-made refried beans with guacamole and tortilla crisps

Preparation time: 20 minutes
(plus overnight soaking)
Cooking time: 1 hour 15 minutes
Serves 4

1 cup dried pinto beans, soaked in cold water overnight

1 tablespoon olive oil

1 large red onion, finely chopped

3 garlic cloves, crushed

1 long red chili, finely chopped

1 teaspoon ground cumin

1 large vine-ripened tomato, coarsely chopped

Cilantro leaves, to garnish

Corn tortilla crisps, to serve

GUACAMOLE

1 firm ripe avocado, stone removed, peeled and diced

3 scallions, white part only, thinly sliced

1 tablespoon finely chopped cilantro

1 long green chili, seeded and finely chopped

Lime juice, to taste

1 Put the pinto beans in a large saucepan and cover with cold water. Bring to the boil, then reduce the heat to low and simmer for 45 minutes–1 hour or until very tender. Drain and set aside.

2 Meanwhile, to make the guacamole, put the avocado in a medium bowl and mash with a fork, leaving some texture. Add the scallions, cilantro, chili, lime juice, and a large pinch of sea salt and stir to combine. Set aside.

3 Heat the olive oil in a large saucepan over medium heat. Add the onion and cook, stirring, for 5 minutes or until softened. Add the garlic, chili, and cumin and cook, stirring, for 1 minute or until fragrant. Add the tomato and cook, stirring, for 2–3 minutes.

4 Add the cooked pinto beans and ¼ cup water. Cook for 5 minutes or until heated through. Use a potato masher to mash the beans, leaving some texture. Season to taste with sea salt and freshly ground black pepper.

5 Serve the beans with the guacamole and tortilla crisps, garnished with cilantro.

These sliders are healthier than most versions, which tend to contain a lot of added sugar. The pork also makes a delicious filling for burritos or tacos.

Pulled pork and black bean sliders with green chili salsa

Preparation time: 25 minutes
Cooking time: 2 hours 15 minutes
Makes 12

1 tablespoon olive oil

2 lb 4 oz piece pork neck

2 onions, coarsely chopped

2 long red chilies, seeded and finely chopped

4 garlic cloves, thinly sliced

2 teaspoons sweet paprika

2 teaspoons ground cumin

1 teaspoon ground coriander

2 cups tomato passata (puréed tomatoes)

1 tablespoon balsamic vinegar

1 tablespoon maple syrup

1 fresh bay leaf

14-oz can black beans, drained and rinsed (see tips)

12 bread rolls, warmed, to serve

Butter lettuce leaves, to serve

GREEN CHILI SALSA
½ cup cilantro leaves
½ cup flat-leaf (Italian) parsley leaves
2 long green chilies, seeded and coarsely chopped
1 tablespoon lime juice
1 tablespoon olive oil

1 Preheat the oven to 325°F. Heat 2 teaspoons of the oil in a large flameproof casserole dish over high heat. Add the pork and cook for 1–2 minutes each side or until browned all over. Remove from the dish and set aside.

2 Return the dish to medium heat, add the remaining oil and the onion, chili, and garlic, and cook, stirring, for 5 minutes or until softened. Add the paprika, cumin, and coriander and cook, stirring, for 1 minute or until fragrant. Return the pork to the pan with the tomato passata, balsamic vinegar, maple syrup, bay leaf, and 1 cup water. Stir to combine and bring to the boil. Cover, transfer to the oven, and bake for 1¾ –2 hours or until the pork is very tender.

3 Meanwhile, to make the green chili salsa, process the cilantro, parsley, and chilies in a food processor until finely chopped. Add the lime juice and olive oil and process until well combined. Season to taste with sea salt.

4 Remove the pork from the dish and set aside to cool slightly. Use two forks to shred the meat. Return the pork to the dish with the black beans and simmer over medium heat for 5 minutes or until heated through. Serve the pork and black beans in warm rolls with the salsa and butter lettuce leaves.

tips You can replace the canned black beans with 1½ cups cooked black beans.

The pulled pork (without the rolls or salsa) is suitable to freeze. Put it in airtight containers, cool completely, cover, and freeze for up to 2 months.

gluten-free (see tips)

This delicious and nutritious meal is so quick and easy to prepare. The chorizo adds a flavor kick, and the beans and rice together provide a complete protein. For a vegetarian version, simply omit the chorizo and replace it with $1^2/_3$ cups sliced button mushrooms.

Chorizo, rice, and bean bowl

Preparation time: 15 minutes
Cooking time: 15 minutes
Serves 4

2 teaspoons olive oil

1 red onion, finely chopped

1 large chorizo
(about $5^1/_2$ oz), diced

1 teaspoon sweet paprika

1 red bell pepper, seeded and diced

2 sweetcorn cobs, kernels removed

14-oz can red kidney beans, drained and rinsed (see tips)

2 cups cooked brown rice (see tips)

3 cups loosely packed trimmed kale (center veins removed), leaves chopped

Lime wedges, to serve

Plain (natural) yogurt, to serve

1 Heat the olive oil in a large saucepan over medium heat. Add the onion and chorizo and cook, stirring, for 5 minutes or until the chorizo is golden. Add the paprika and cook, stirring, for 1 minute or until fragrant.

2 Add the bell pepper and corn kernels and cook, stirring, for 2 minutes or until almost tender. Add the beans and rice and cook for 2 minutes or until heated through. Add the kale and cook, stirring, until just wilted.

3 Serve with a wedge of lime and a dollop of yogurt.

tips For a gluten-free version, use gluten-free chorizo.

You can replace the canned kidney beans with $1^1/_2$ cups cooked kidney beans, and you can replace the kale with trimmed Swiss chard or spinach leaves.

To make 2 cups cooked brown rice, start with $^3/_4$ cup uncooked.

dairy-free • gluten-free (see tips)

This is a much simpler and lighter version of the traditional hearty Brazilian black bean stew, but it is still packed with flavor. Traditionally it contains a combination of smoked, fresh, and salted meats.

Feijoada (Brazilian black bean stew)

Preparation time: 15 minutes
(plus overnight soaking)
Cooking time: 3 hours 15 minutes
Serves 6

1 tablespoon olive oil

14 oz pork ribs, rind removed, cut into chunks (see tips)

1 chorizo, thinly sliced

2 onions, thinly sliced

4 garlic cloves, crushed

14-oz can diced tomatoes

1⅓ cups dried black beans, soaked in cold water overnight

9 oz corned beef, cut into chunks (see tips)

3 fresh bay leaves

Steamed rice, to serve

Coarsely chopped flat-leaf (Italian) parsley, to garnish

1 Heat two teaspoons of the oil in a large heavy-bottomed frying pan over medium heat. Add the pork ribs and cook, turning, for 2–3 minutes or until golden. Add the chorizo and cook for 2 minutes or until browned. Remove from the pan and set aside.

2 Return the pan to medium heat. Add the remaining oil and the onion and cook, stirring, for 5 minutes or until golden. Add the garlic and cook, stirring, for 1 minute. Add the pork ribs, chorizo, tomatoes, beans, corned beef, bay leaves, and 2 cups water.

3 Cover and simmer over low heat, stirring occasionally, for 2½–3 hours or until the beans and meats are very tender and the stew is thick. Serve with rice, garnished with parsley.

tips For a gluten-free version, use gluten-free chorizo and corned beef.

Corned beef is available from butchers and from the refrigerated meat section of supermarkets.

You can replace the pork ribs with pork belly, rind removed.

This stew is suitable to freeze. Put it in airtight containers, cool completely, cover, and freeze for up to 2 months.

Legumes are a great addition to curries and stews. They reduce the amount of meat needed and lower the cost of the meal – perfect for families.

Masala beef and red kidney bean curry

Preparation time: 20 minutes
(plus overnight soaking)
Cooking time: 1 hour 45 minutes
Serves 4

1½ tablespoons olive oil

14 oz chuck (blade) steak, trimmed and cut into ¾-inch cubes

1 cinnamon stick

2 fresh bay leaves

2 onions, thinly sliced

⅓ cup tikka masala curry paste

14-oz can diced tomatoes

1 cup dried red kidney beans, soaked in cold water overnight

½ cup plain (natural) yogurt

Fresh cilantro leaves, to garnish (optional)

Lime wedges, to garnish

Steamed greens, such as broccolini, to serve

1 Preheat the oven to 325°F. Heat 2 teaspoons of the oil in a large flameproof casserole dish over high heat. Add half the beef and cook, turning, for 2–3 minutes or until golden. Remove from the dish and set aside. Repeat with another 2 teaspoons of the oil and the remaining beef.

2 Return the dish to medium heat. Add the remaining 2 teaspoons of oil, the cinnamon stick, and the bay leaves and cook, stirring, for 1 minute or until fragrant. Add the sliced onion and cook, stirring occasionally, for 5 minutes or until golden. Add the curry paste and cook, stirring, for 1 minute or until fragrant.

3 Return the beef to the pan. Add the tomatoes, kidney beans, and 2 cups water and bring to the boil. Cover, transfer to oven, and bake for 1½ hours or until the beef and beans are very tender. Stir in the yogurt and serve garnished with cilantro leaves (if desired) and lime wedges, accompanied by steamed greens.

tips For a gluten-free version, use gluten-free curry paste.

The curry, excluding the yogurt, is suitable to freeze. Put it in airtight containers and cool completely. Cover and freeze for up to 2 months.

» pictured pages 154–155

Masala beef and red kidney bean curry

(see recipe page 153)

Yogurt flat breads

(see recipe page 190)

Black beans can work beautifully in chocolate baked goods and desserts. They add body, texture, protein, and fiber, and they can be used to replace some of the butter or flour (or both) in recipes. Yogurt is the perfect accompaniment to this cake, and a much healthier choice than cream. Coconut sugar has a delicious caramel flavor.

Flourless chocolate dessert cake with raspberry yogurt cream

Preparation time: 20 minutes
Cooking time: 40 minutes
Serves 10–12

14-oz can black beans, drained and rinsed (see tip)

4 eggs

1 teaspoon pure vanilla extract

¾ cup coconut sugar

⅓ cup unsalted butter, softened

⅓ cup unsweetened cocoa powder, plus extra (optional) for dusting

1 teaspoon baking powder

½ cup hazelnut meal

½ cup fresh or frozen raspberries

RASPBERRY YOGURT CREAM
1 cup plain (natural) yogurt
½ cup fresh or frozen raspberries
2 teaspoons honey
1 teaspoon pure vanilla extract

1 Preheat the oven to 325°F. Lightly grease an 8-inch round non-stick springform cake pan. Process the black beans in a food processor until almost smooth. Add the eggs one at a time, and the vanilla, and process until completely smooth.

2 Use an electric mixer to beat the sugar and butter until pale and creamy. Stir in the bean mixture (the mixture will appear curdled).

3 Sift the cocoa, baking powder, and a pinch of salt together. Gently fold into the bean mixture with the hazelnut meal. Stir in the raspberries.

4 Spoon the mixture into the prepared pan and smooth the surface with the back of the spoon. Bake for 35–40 minutes or until a skewer inserted into the center comes out clean. Set aside to cool for 5 minutes. Remove from the pan and set aside on a wire rack to cool completely. Dust with extra cocoa if desired.

5 Meanwhile, to make the raspberry yogurt cream, place all the ingredients in a small bowl and stir to combine. Serve with the chocolate cake.

tip You can replace the canned black beans with 1½ cups cooked black beans, red kidney beans, adzuki beans, or pinto beans, and the coconut sugar with brown sugar.

lentils

lentils

LENTILS HAVE BEEN PART of the human diet for some 13,000 years and were one of the first crops to be domesticated. These small lens-shaped seeds not only come in many colors and sizes, but pack a big nutritional punch.

They are sold in various forms, with or without the skins, whole or split. Lentils with their skins tend to remain intact during cooking, while lentils without their skin tend to disintegrate into a thick purée, leading to quite different dishes. Whole lentils are good for salads, pasta, and vegetable dishes, while split lentils are used for soups and purées.

Lentils have a distinctive earthy flavor and naturally lend themselves to being cooked with assertive flavors such as onion, garlic, chili, dried spices, and fresh herbs. They are frequently combined with rice, which has a similar cooking time, and in this combination they provide a complete protein, with all the essential amino acids.

Lentils range in color from yellow and red to green, brown, and even black. Green lentils are larger and flatter than other varieties, retain their shape and firmness after cooking, do not easily break down with stirring, and work beautifully in salads, soups,

French green lentils, or Puy lentils, from the region of Le Puy in France, are smaller and darker than other lentils and are considered to have a superior flavor. They require an extended cooking time, around 25 minutes.

Brown lentils hold their shape well during cooking but can become mushy if overcooked. This variety cooks in about 20 minutes and requires no soaking. Brown lentils are ideal for soups, stews, and pilafs. They can be purchased canned, which makes them very convenient, and there is negligible difference in nutritional content between canned and dried lentils.

Yellow lentils are sweet and nutty. Hulled and split, they tend to break down quickly with cooking and are best suited to dishes that require thickening. Also known as moong dal, they are traditional in Indian recipes such as dal, where they are cooked down to a smooth purée. They can also be ground into flour and used to make poppadoms or combined with other flours to make breads and cakes.

Red lentils are also hulled and split, and they are the quickest to cook, although not as nutritious as the green and brown varieties. They are popular in curries and are also used to make dal and a variety of

Lentils are nutritional powerhouses. Their protein content is among the highest of any legume, topped only by soy beans, making them an essential source of inexpensive protein in many parts of the world. They are also packed with dietary fiber, both soluble and insoluble, which not only assists in reducing cholesterol levels, but can also help stabilize and regulate blood sugar levels. Lentils are a rich source of folate and magnesium.

Inexpensive, naturally gluten- and dairy-free, easy to store without refrigeration, and quick to cook, it is little wonder lentils are a staple food in many cultures.

Cooking instructions

The manufacturers of some pressure cookers recommend against cooking split lentils by this method because they tend to foam and splutter and can clog the valve. Check the instruction manual provided with your pressure cooker.

PUY (FRENCH GREEN) LENTILS
Stovetop
Rinse and drain 1 cup Puy lentils. Put them in a large saucepan with 6 cups water and bring to the boil. Reduce the heat and simmer for 25–30 minutes or until just tender. Drain.

Pressure cooker
Rinse and drain 1 cup Puy lentils. Cook with 4 cups water at high pressure for 10–12 minutes or until tender. Drain.

BROWN OR GREEN LENTILS
Stovetop
Rinse and drain 1 cup brown or green lentils. Put them in a large saucepan with 6 cups water and bring to the boil. Reduce heat and simmer for 20–25 minutes or until just tender. Drain.

Pressure cooker
Rinse and drain 1 cup brown lentils. Cook with 4 cups water at high pressure for 8–10 minutes or until just tender. Drain.

RED SPLIT LENTILS
Stovetop
Rinse and drain 1 cup red split lentils. Put them in a large saucepan with 3 cups cold water and bring to the boil. Reduce the heat and simmer for 15–20 minutes or until thick. The lentils will have a dal-like consistency.

Pressure cooker
Rinse and drain 1 cup red split lentils. Cook with 4 cups water at high pressure for 5–10 minutes or until thick.

YELLOW SPLIT LENTILS (MOONG DAL)
Stovetop
Rinse and drain 1 cup yellow split lentils. Put them in a large saucepan with 3 cups cold water and bring to the boil. Reduce the heat and simmer for 30 minutes or until thick.

Pressure cooker
Rinse and drain 1 cup yellow split lentils. Cook with 4 cups water at high pressure for 5–10 minutes or until thick.

NUTRITION	PER 100 G (3½ OZ) COOKED RED OR YELLOW SPLIT LENTILS	PER 100 G (3½ OZ) COOKED BROWN, GREEN, OR FRENCH GREEN LENTILS
Energy	109 cal	142 cal
Protein	7.7 g	10 g
Fat	0.6 g	0.8 g
Saturated fat	0.1 g	0.1 g
Carbohydrate	16.4 g	20.2 g
Dietary fiber	2.2 g	5.2 g
Iron	1.4 mg	2.3 mg
Folate	20 µg	28 µg
Magnesium	18 mg	31 mg

vegan • gluten-free (see tips)

Roasting the tomatoes concentrates their natural sweetness and adds depth of flavor to the soup. Red lentils are extremely nutritious, packed with plant protein and dietary fiber. Even better, they don't require soaking, and will cook in less than 20 minutes.

Roasted tomato and lentil soup

Preparation time: 15 minutes
Cooking time: 45 minutes
Serves 4

12–14 roma (plum) tomatoes, halved
2 teaspoons thyme leaves
2 teaspoons balsamic vinegar
1 tablespoon olive oil
1 large red onion, finely chopped
2 celery stalks, trimmed and diced
2 garlic cloves, crushed
2 cups low-sodium vegetable stock
½ cup red lentils, rinsed and drained
Basil leaves, to serve

1 Preheat the oven to 350°F. Line a large baking tray with parchment paper. Place the tomatoes cut-side up on the prepared tray. Sprinkle with the thyme, drizzle with the balsamic vinegar, and season to taste with sea salt and freshly ground black pepper. Roast for 30 minutes or until extremely tender. Set aside.

2 Meanwhile, heat the olive oil in a large saucepan over medium heat. Add the onion and celery and cook, stirring, for 5 minutes or until softened. Add the garlic and cook for 30 seconds or until fragrant.

3 Add the stock and lentils, cover and simmer for 10 minutes, stirring occasionally. Add the roasted tomatoes, cover, and simmer for 10 minutes or until the lentils are tender. Set aside to cool slightly.

4 Blend the soup in batches until smooth. Return the soup to a clean saucepan and heat over medium heat. Season to taste with sea salt and freshly ground black pepper. Serve garnished with basil.

tips For a gluten-free version, use gluten-free stock.

Before cooking the lentils, it is important to rinse them until the water runs clear. This prevents excessive scum from forming on the surface of the cooking liquid.

This soup freezes beautifully. Put it in airtight containers, cool completely, cover, and freeze for up to 2 months.

» **pictured page 164**

vegetarian

Canned brown lentils are quick and convenient, and there's negligible difference in nutritional content between the canned and dried versions. These super-healthy fritters are packed with vegetables and fiber and are a good source of protein. They make a filling lunch or a lighter dinner.

Zucchini, lentil, and haloumi fritters with tzatziki

Preparation time: 15 minutes
Cooking time: 30 minutes
Serves 4

½ small head broccoli, trimmed and cut into florets

14-oz can brown lentils, drained and rinsed

2 zucchini, coarsely grated (about 1½ cups, firmly packed), squeezed to remove excess moisture

2 eggs, lightly beaten

½ cup self-raising flour

2¾ oz haloumi cheese, grated

¼ cup finely chopped mint

2 tablespoons snipped chives

Finely grated zest of 1 lemon

1 tablespoon olive oil

Tzatziki, to serve (see tips)

Lemon wedges, to serve

Baby spinach leaves, to serve

1 Cook the broccoli in a saucepan of boiling water for 3–4 minutes or until tender. Drain and transfer to a large bowl.

2 Roughly mash the broccoli with a fork. Add the lentils, zucchini, eggs, flour, haloumi, mint, chives, and lemon zest and stir to combine. Season to taste with sea salt and freshly ground black pepper.

3 Heat the olive oil in a large non-stick frying pan over medium–high heat. Add 3 x ¼-cups of mixture and cook the fritters for 2–3 minutes each side or until golden and cooked through (see tips). Repeat with the remaining batter, adding a little extra oil if necessary.

4 Serve the fritters with tzatziki, lemon wedges, and baby spinach leaves.

tips For a gluten-free version, replace the self-raising flour with gluten-free self-raising flour.

To ensure that the fritters hold together when they're flipped, it is important to cook them until they're completely golden on one side first.

To make your own tzatziki, grate 1 Lebanese (short) cucumber and combine it with ½ cup plain yogurt, 1 crushed garlic clove, and a squeeze of lemon juice.

» **pictured page 165**

Roasted tomato and lentil soup

(see recipe page 162)

Zucchini, lentil, and haloumi fritters with tzatziki

(see recipe page 163)

vegetarian • gluten-free

Puy lentils (French green lentils) are smaller and darker than regular green lentils. They retain their shape and firmness after cooking, and therefore work beautifully in salads.

Roasted beet, lentil, and goat's feta salad with caramelized seeds

Preparation time: 20 minutes
Cooking time: 1 hour
Serves 4

About 6 baby beets, trimmed

1 cup dried Puy lentils, rinsed and drained

1 shallot, finely chopped

1 tablespoon red wine vinegar

2 celery stalks, trimmed and finely chopped

2 tablespoons coarsely chopped flat-leaf (Italian) parsley

2 tablespoons coarsely chopped mint

2 cups baby spinach leaves

1¾ oz (50 g) marinated goat's feta

CARAMELIZED SEEDS

2 tablespoons pepitas (pumpkin seeds)

2 tablespoons sunflower seeds

1 teaspoon brown sugar

1 teaspoon honey

½ teaspoon ground cinnamon

1 Preheat the oven to 400°F. Place the beets on a large baking tray, cover the tray with foil, and roast for 1 hour or until the beets are tender when pierced with a skewer. Set aside to cool slightly, then peel (see tip) and cut into wedges.

2 Meanwhile, cook the lentils in a saucepan of boiling water for 25 minutes or until just tender. Drain. Transfer to a large bowl and add the shallot and vinegar. Set aside to cool. Add the celery, parsley, and mint. Season to taste with sea salt and freshly ground black pepper. Set aside.

3 To make the caramelized seeds, put all the ingredients in a bowl and toss to combine. Spread in a single layer on a small baking tray lined with parchment paper. Roast for 5–10 minutes or until golden and caramelized. Set aside to cool.

4 To serve, add the beets and spinach to the lentil mixture and toss to combine. Arrange the salad on a serving plate, crumble the goat's feta over the top, and sprinkle with the caramelized seeds.

tip Wear gloves when peeling the beets to prevent your hands from being stained.

Lentils of all types are packed with dietary fiber, both soluble and insoluble, which not only assists in reducing cholesterol levels, but can help stabilize and regulate blood sugar levels.

Puy lentil, asparagus, and fava bean salad with pickled onions and dukkah

Preparation time: 20 minutes
Cooking time: 30 minutes
Serves 4

1¾ cups shelled fresh or frozen fava beans

⅔ cup dried Puy lentils, rinsed and drained

2 tablespoons red wine vinegar

1 tablespoon olive oil

1 small red onion, thinly sliced

½ teaspoon granulated sugar

¼ teaspoon sea salt

8 asparagus spears, trimmed and cut into 1½-inch lengths

7 oz green beans, trimmed and halved

2 cups loosely packed pea shoots or watercress leaves

4 eggs

1 tablespoon almond dukkah (see tips)

Flat bread, to serve

1 Cook the fava beans in a saucepan of boiling water for 3 minutes or until tender. Refresh under cold running water. Drain. Peel off the skins and discard. Set aside.

2 Cook the lentils in a saucepan of boiling water for 25 minutes or until al dente. Drain and transfer to a large bowl. Add 1 tablespoon of the vinegar and the olive oil, season to taste with sea salt and freshly ground black pepper, stir to combine, and set aside to cool.

3 Combine the onion, remaining vinegar, sugar, and salt in a small bowl. Set aside to pickle for 5 minutes.

4 Meanwhile, cook the asparagus and green beans in boiling water until just tender. Refresh and drain. Add the asparagus, green beans, fava beans, and pea shoots to the lentils. Toss to combine.

5 Place the eggs in a saucepan and cover with cold water. Bring to the boil, then reduce the heat to low–medium and simmer for 4 minutes for soft-boiled eggs. Drain, peel, and cut in half.

6 Divide the salad between plates and top each with some pickled onions and an egg. Sprinkle with dukkah and serve with flat bread.

tips For a gluten-free version, use gluten-free flat bread.

If you're using frozen fava beans, you can skip the initial cooking (step 1). Simply place them in a large bowl, cover with warm water, set aside for 10 minutes, then peel.

Dukkah is an Egyptian blend of spices, dried herbs, and roasted nuts. You can find it in the spice section of most supermarkets.

Replacing half the usual amount of meat in a bolognese sauce with lentils is a great way to increase the vegetable content and reduce the cost of the meal. For a vegetarian version, omit the pork and double the quantity of lentils.

Lentil bolognese

Preparation time: 15 minutes
Cooking time: 35 minutes
Serves 4

1 tablespoon olive oil

1 onion, finely chopped

1 small carrot, peeled and finely chopped

1 celery stalk, finely chopped

1 small zucchini, trimmed and finely chopped

2 garlic cloves, crushed

2 teaspoons finely chopped rosemary

9 oz minced (ground) pork

2 tablespoons unsalted tomato paste (concentrated purée)

½ cup white wine

14-oz can diced tomatoes

14-oz can brown lentils, drained and rinsed (see tips)

3 cups whole-wheat pasta, such as wholemeal spelt

Freshly grated parmesan cheese, to serve

1 Heat the olive oil in a large saucepan over medium heat. Add the onion, carrot, and celery and cook, stirring, for 6–7 minutes or until softened. Add the zucchini, garlic, and rosemary and cook, stirring, for 1 minute. Add the pork and cook, breaking up the meat with a wooden spoon, for 4–5 minutes or until browned.

2 Add the tomato paste and cook, stirring, for 1 minute. Add the wine and simmer until reduced by half. Add the tomatoes and ⅓ cup water and bring to the boil. Reduce the heat to low and simmer for 10 minutes. Add the lentils and simmer for 10 minutes or until thick. Season to taste with sea salt and freshly ground black pepper.

3 Meanwhile, cook the pasta in a large saucepan of lightly salted boiling water according to the package instructions or until al dente. Drain well, return to the pan with the sauce, and toss until well combined. Divide the pasta between bowls and serve with parmesan.

tips For a gluten-free version, use gluten-free pasta.

You can replace the canned lentils with 1½ cups cooked lentils.

This bolognese is suitable to freeze. Put it in airtight containers, cool completely, cover, and freeze for up to 2 months.

Lentil and quinoa pilaf with roasted vegetables

(see recipe page 172)

Of all the legumes, lentils are among the highest in protein. Combined with quinoa, they make a high-protein vegetarian dish that's packed with flavor and fiber as well as being a rich source of folate and magnesium.

Lentil and quinoa pilaf with roasted vegetables

Preparation time: 15 minutes
Cooking time: 40 minutes
Serves 4

½ cup dried brown or green lentils, rinsed and drained

½ small head cauliflower, trimmed and cut into florets

1 red bell pepper, seeded and sliced

Olive oil spray, for coating

1 head broccoli, trimmed and cut into florets

1 tablespoon olive oil

1 onion, finely chopped

2 garlic cloves, crushed

1 teaspoon cumin seeds, crushed

1 cinnamon stick

1 cup low-sodium vegetable or chicken stock

½ cup quinoa, rinsed and drained

¼ cup coarsely chopped flat-leaf (Italian) parsley

Plain (natural) yogurt, to serve

2 tablespoons shelled unsalted pistachios, coarsely chopped

Thinly sliced lemon zest, to garnish

1 Place the lentils in a medium saucepan and cover with cold water. Bring to the boil over high heat, then reduce the heat to low–medium and simmer for 20–25 minutes or until tender. Drain.

2 Meanwhile, preheat the oven to 400°F. Line a large baking tray with parchment paper. Put the cauliflower and bell pepper on the prepared tray and spray lightly with olive oil. Roast for 10 minutes. Add the broccoli to the tray and spray with a little more oil. Roast for 10 minutes or until the vegetables are golden and tender. Set aside.

3 Heat the oil in a large saucepan over medium heat. Add the onion and cook, stirring, for 5 minutes or until light golden. Add the garlic, cumin, and cinnamon and cook, stirring, for 1 minute or until fragrant. Add the stock and quinoa and bring to the boil. Cover and simmer for 12–15 minutes or until the stock has been absorbed and the quinoa is al dente. Stir in the lentils and parsley.

4 Serve the lentil and quinoa pilaf topped with the roasted vegetables and a dollop of yogurt, garnished with pistachios and a little lemon zest.

« pictured pages 170–171

Moong dal are skinned yellow split lentils with a sweet and nutty taste. They tend to break down quickly with cooking and are ideal for dishes that require thickening, such as dal.

Spinach and lentil dal

Preparation time: 15 minutes
Cooking time: 35 minutes
Serves 4

2 tablespoons sunflower oil or ghee

1 brown onion, finely chopped

1 cup dried yellow split lentils (moong dal)

2 vine-ripened tomatoes, diced

Pinch of cayenne pepper

1 teaspoon brown mustard seeds

10 fresh curry leaves

1 teaspoon garam masala

3 garlic cloves, crushed

1 teaspoon finely grated ginger

2 long green chilies, seeded and chopped

1 bunch spinach, trimmed and shredded

1 Heat 2 teaspoons of the oil in a large saucepan over medium heat. Add the onion and cook, stirring, for 2 minutes. Add the lentils, tomatoes, cayenne pepper, and 3 cups cold water and bring to the boil. Reduce the heat to low and simmer for 30 minutes or until the lentils are very soft and starting to break up, adding a little extra water if necessary.

2 Heat the remaining oil in a small saucepan over medium heat. Add the mustard seeds and curry leaves and cook, stirring, for 30 seconds or until the seeds start to pop. Add the garam masala, garlic, ginger, and chilies and cook, stirring, for 1 minute.

3 Add the spice mixture and spinach to the lentils and stir to combine. Cook for 1–2 minutes or until the spinach has just wilted. Serve immediately.

tips It is important to serve the dal as soon as the spinach is added, so it stays vibrant and fresh.

The dal is suitable to freeze without the spinach. Put it in an airtight container and cool completely. Cover and freeze for up to 2 months.

This dish is definitely worthy of a dinner party. The lentils can be made ahead of time then gently reheated after your guests have arrived. Bitter salad leaves cut through the richness of the duck, making the perfect accompaniment.

Duck breast with pancetta, braised lentils, and balsamic

Preparation time: 15 minutes
Cooking time: 35 minutes
Serves 4

4 small duck breasts (about 4½ oz each), skin on

1 teaspoon brown sugar

1 teaspoon fennel seeds, lightly crushed

½ teaspoon sea salt

Bitter salad leaves, such as chicory or endive, to serve

Balsamic vinegar, to drizzle

BRAISED LENTILS

2 teaspoons olive oil

2 shallots, finely chopped

1 celery stalk, finely chopped

2¾ oz pancetta, diced

2 garlic cloves, crushed

2 teaspoons chopped thyme

2 cups low-sodium chicken stock

1 cup dried Puy lentils, rinsed and drained

1 fresh bay leaf

2 teaspoons balsamic vinegar

1 To make the braised lentils, heat the olive oil in a medium saucepan over medium heat. Add the shallots, celery, and pancetta and cook, stirring, for 5 minutes or until softened. Add the crushed garlic and thyme and cook, stirring, for 1 minute or until fragrant. Add the stock, lentils, and bay leaf and bring to the boil. Reduce the heat to low and simmer partially covered, stirring occasionally, for 25–30 minutes or until the lentils are tender. Stir in the balsamic vinegar and keep warm.

2 Meanwhile, preheat the oven to 350°F. Using a sharp knife, score the skin of each duck breast 5–6 times. Combine the sugar, fennel seeds, and salt in a small bowl. Rub the sugar mixture evenly into the skin of each breast.

3 Heat a large frying pan over medium heat. Add the duck, skin-side down, and cook for 6–7 minutes or until the skin is crisp and the fat has rendered. Turn and cook for another minute. Transfer the duck to a large baking tray and roast for 5 minutes. Remove from the oven, cover loosely with foil, and set aside to rest for 5 minutes.

4 To serve, thinly slice the duck. Serve on the braised lentils with some bitter salad leaves, drizzled with balsamic vinegar.

tips For a gluten-free version, use gluten-free stock and pancetta.

It is important to cook the duck skin-side down over medium (not high) heat so the fat has time to render and the skin doesn't burn.

peanuts
& lupins

peanuts & lupins

Peanuts and lupins are perhaps most often thought of as nuts and cottage garden flowers respectively, but in fact both are legumes. As such, they share many valuable nutritional and dietary features, including their high levels of protein, dietary fiber, and disease-fighting antioxidants. Note that people who are allergic to peanuts may also experience a reaction to lupins.

peanuts

DESPITE ITS NAME and appearance, the peanut is not a nut, but rather a member of the legume family. The culinary use of peanuts, however, does closely resemble that of nuts.

The plant grows to 12–20 inches tall, and when the flowers have been pollinated the flower stalks bend and grow into the ground. The fruit develops underground into a legume pod, the peanut.

Peanuts are incredibly diverse in the kitchen, working beautifully in both savory and sweet recipes, and they can be eaten raw, boiled, roasted, salted, or sweetened. They are used in sauces including the ever-popular satay sauce, in snack foods such as muesli bars, or ground into peanut butter and used as a spread. Peanuts can be added to salads, stir-fries, candy, baked goods, and desserts, or pressed to yield peanut oil.

Peanut oil is useful in cooking because it has a mild flavor and a relatively high smoke point, which makes it ideal for frying. It has a high monounsaturated fat content and is considered healthier than saturated oils.

Peanuts are rich in nutrients. As well as having a high protein content (around 20%), they contain considerably more fat than most legumes. They are rich in healthy monounsaturated fats, which can help to lower cholesterol. They are a good source of niacin, folate, fiber, vitamin E, magnesium, copper, and zinc, and a significant source of antioxidants, particularly resveratrol, an antioxidant thought to be associated with a reduced risk of cardiovascular disease.

Some people experience a mild to severe allergic reaction to peanut exposure: symptoms range from watery eyes to anaphylactic shock, which can be life-threatening if untreated. For this reason, many schools and pre-schools have banned foods containing peanuts from lunchboxes.

Cooking instructions

To roast raw peanuts, preheat the oven to 350°F. Spread 1 cup peanuts evenly on a baking tray. Roast for 8–10 minutes or until golden. Alternatively, cook in a dry frying pan over medium heat, stirring often, for 4–5 minutes or until golden.

NUTRITION	PER 35 G (1¼ OZ/ ¼ CUP) RAW PEANUTS	PER 100 G (3½ OZ) RAW PEANUTS
Energy	222 cal	570 cal
Protein	10 g	24.7 g
Fat	17.1 g	47.1 g
Saturated fat	2.6 g	7.1 g
Carbohydrate	5.3 g	10.1 g
Dietary fiber	4.9 g	8.2 g
Vitamin E	3.4 mg	9.5 mg
Folate	111.6 µg	240 µg
Magnesium	70.6 mg	160 mg
Zinc	1.7 mg	3 mg

lupins

LUPINS ARE ONE OF THE less well known members of the legume family. They have been consumed throughout the Mediterranean region and the Andean mountains for thousands of years, but have been known for their bitter taste, which comes from alkaloids. Modern plant breeders, however, have cultivated sweet lupins through selective breeding.

Researchers and nutritionists believe that the new varieties of sweet lupins have great potential, are superior to soy beans in certain applications, and are possibly "the next big thing" in human nutrition.

With a protein content of around 40%, lupins are one of the richest sources of plant protein, and they are packed with dietary fiber (more than 30%). They're also rich in antioxidants, low in carbohydrates and fat, and naturally gluten-free. Research suggests that lupin-enriched diets have a role in decreasing blood pressure and improving glucose metabolism (insulin sensitivity), and that their low GI and high fiber content may help with appetite control.

Dried lupins require soaking before cooking, and then they can be boiled until tender. Fresh lupin seeds have a taste and texture similar to those of field peas and can be used in salads, stir-fries, and pickles. Currently, the most readily available form of lupins is lupin flour, which is available from selected health food stores. It can be used in recipes that call for wheat flour, such as bread, muffins, other baked goods, and even pasta.

Try replacing 20–50% of the wheat flour in recipes with lupin flour. This will not only increase the protein and fiber content considerably, but will reduce the overall energy density and glycemic index of the finished product. Lupin flour is therefore excellent for people with diabetes or those following a low-GI diet.

It is important to note that people who are allergic to peanuts may also suffer a reaction to lupins.

If you are unable to find lupin flour, besan (chickpea flour) works well in most recipes that contain lupin flour. Besan flour is low GI, gluten-free, and rich in protein. It is a soft yellow color and, like lupin flour, has a distinctive aroma that dissipates once cooked.

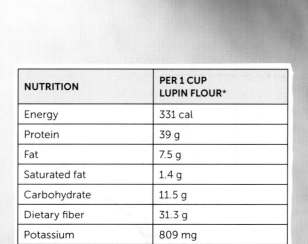

NUTRITION	PER 1 CUP LUPIN FLOUR*
Energy	331 cal
Protein	39 g
Fat	7.5 g
Saturated fat	1.4 g
Carbohydrate	11.5 g
Dietary fiber	31.3 g
Potassium	809 mg

* Accredited nutritional analysis for lupin flour is unavailable because of lupins' small production and relatively recent availability.

Rolled oats and barley are both packed with beta glucan soluble fiber, which has been proven to help lower cholesterol and therefore may possibly reduce the risk of heart attack. Their high protein and fiber content helps to keep you feeling full for longer, which makes this granola perfect for breakfast.

Peanut, maple, and seed granola

Preparation time: 15 minutes
Cooking time: 30 minutes
Makes 4 cups

1 cup rolled oats

1 cup barley flakes

½ cup buckwheat groats (kasha)

½ cup unsalted raw peanuts

2 tablespoons pepitas (pumpkin seeds)

2 tablespoons sunflower seeds

1 tablespoon chia seeds

1 teaspoon ground cinnamon

2½ tablespoons maple syrup

2 teaspoons macadamia oil or peanut oil

1 teaspoon pure vanilla extract

½ cup mixed dried fruit, such as sweetened dried cranberries and dried figs, coarsely chopped

½ cup toasted coconut flakes

1 Preheat the oven to 300°F. Line a large baking tray with parchment paper.

2 Combine the oats, barley, buckwheat, peanuts, pepitas, sunflower seeds, chia seeds, and cinnamon in a large bowl. Add the maple syrup, oil, and vanilla and toss to coat. Spread the mixture evenly on the prepared tray.

3 Bake, stirring every 10 minutes, for 25 minutes or until light golden and crisp. Stir in the coconut flakes and bake for a further 5 minutes or until the granola is golden. Stir in the dried fruit and set aside to cool completely.

tip The granola will keep in an airtight container for up to 1 month.

This salad is fresh, light, and full of flavor. To make a more substantial meal, add half a cup of steamed brown rice or quinoa per person.

Spicy chicken salad with peanuts, cabbage, and mint

Preparation time: 20 minutes
Cooking time: 5 minutes
Serves 4

½ small red cabbage, trimmed and shredded

1 cup cherry tomatoes, halved

½ cup mint leaves

½ cup cilantro leaves

⅓ cup unsalted roasted peanuts, coarsely chopped

14 oz minced (ground) chicken (see tips)

1 lemongrass stem, pale part only, finely chopped

2 red Asian shallots, finely chopped

2 teaspoons peanut oil

DRESSING

2 tablespoons lime juice

1 tablespoon fish sauce

3 teaspoons brown sugar

1–2 long red chilies, or to taste, seeded and finely chopped (see tips)

1 To make the dressing, combine the lime juice, fish sauce, sugar, and chili in a small bowl, stirring to dissolve the sugar. Set aside.

2 Combine the cabbage, tomatoes, mint, cilantro, and peanuts in a large bowl. Set aside.

3 Combine the chicken, lemongrass, shallots, and oil in a medium bowl. Heat a wok over high heat. Add the chicken mixture and stir-fry, breaking up the minced chicken, for 2–3 minutes or until golden. Add to the vegetables, drizzle with the dressing, and gently toss to combine. Serve immediately.

tips You can replace the minced chicken with minced turkey, pork, or beef.

If you like things really spicy, replace the long red chilies with 1–2 bird's eye chilies.

» pictured page 184

dairy-free • gluten-free

Marinating the meat before cooking is the secret to these delicious pork satay skewers. Thinly sliced rump steak, chicken breast, or lamb leg steak would work equally well.

Pork satays with pickled carrot salad

Preparation time: 20 minutes
(plus 20 minutes soaking and
1 hour marinating)
Cooking time: 10 minutes
Serves 4

1/3 cup unsalted roasted peanuts

2 tablespoons low-sodium soy sauce

1 tablespoon lemon juice

1 1/2 tablespoons mirin

1 tablespoon curry powder

1 garlic clove, crushed

4 x 4 1/2-oz pork leg steaks, trimmed
and cut into long strips

12 short wooden skewers, soaked in
cold water for 20 minutes (see tip)

Peanut oil, for brushing

1/3 cup coconut milk

PICKLED CARROT SALAD

2 tablespoons rice vinegar

2 teaspoons granulated sugar

2 carrots, peeled and trimmed

2 Lebanese (short) cucumbers, trimmed

1 red apple, cored and cut into
thin matchsticks

1/4 cup cilantro leaves,
roughly chopped

1 Process the peanuts in a food processor until finely chopped. Add the soy sauce, lemon juice, mirin, curry powder, and garlic and process until well combined.

2 Transfer half the peanut mixture to a shallow glass or ceramic dish (reserve the remainder). Add the pork and turn to coat. Cover and set aside in the refrigerator to marinate for at least 1 hour.

3 Meanwhile, to begin the pickled carrot salad, combine the rice vinegar, sugar, and a large pinch of sea salt in a small saucepan and bring to a simmer over medium heat. Remove from the heat and set aside to cool. Transfer to a large bowl. Use a vegetable peeler or mandolin to cut long ribbons or strands from the carrot and cucumber, stopping when you reach the seeds. Add the vegetables to the vinegar mixture and toss to combine. Set aside to pickle for 10 minutes.

4 Thread the pork onto the prepared skewers. Heat a grill pan over high heat and brush with oil. Grill the pork skewers, turning, for 4–5 minutes or until lightly charred and cooked to your liking.

5 Meanwhile, combine the remaining peanut mixture with the coconut milk in a small saucepan. Bring to a simmer over medium heat and simmer for 2 minutes or until slightly thickened.

6 Drain the pickling liquid from the vegetables (discard the liquid) and toss the vegetables with the apple and cilantro. Serve the satays with the peanut sauce and the pickled carrot salad.

tip Soaking wooden skewers in water prevents them from burning. If you're short of time, substitute metal skewers.

» **pictured page 185**

Spicy chicken salad with peanuts, cabbage, and mint

(see recipe page 182)

**Pork satays with
pickled carrot salad**

(see recipe page 183)

vegan

Peanuts add a delicious crunch and an additional source of protein to this vegetarian stir-fry. Broccoli is high in dietary fiber, low in calories, and packed with disease- and cancer-fighting compounds – it's a true superfood.

Stir-fried tofu, broccoli, and peanuts

Preparation time: 15 minutes
Cooking time: 10 minutes
Serves 4

2 tablespoons Chinese rice wine

2 tablespoons low-sodium tamari

2 teaspoons sweet soy sauce

1 teaspoon cornstarch

1 tablespoon peanut oil (see tips)

¼ cup unsalted raw peanuts

12 oz firm tofu, drained and cut into ¾-inch cubes

3 celery stalks, trimmed and sliced

2 garlic cloves, crushed

1 long red chili, seeded and finely chopped

1 large head broccoli, trimmed and cut into florets

1 Combine the Chinese rice wine, tamari, sweet soy sauce, and cornstarch in a small bowl, stirring until smooth. Set aside.

2 Heat half the oil in a large wok over high heat. Add the peanuts and stir-fry for 1 minute or until golden. Remove from the wok and set aside. Add the tofu and stir-fry for 2–3 minutes or until golden. Remove from the wok and set aside with the peanuts.

3 Return the wok to high heat. Add the remaining oil and the celery, garlic, and chili and stir-fry for 1 minute. Add the broccoli and stir-fry for 1–2 minutes or until bright green. Add the tofu, peanuts, and reserved sauces and simmer for 1 minute or until the tofu is heated through and sauce has thickened slightly. Serve immediately.

tips You can replace the broccoli with 2–3 bunches broccolini, trimmed and cut into long florets.

Peanut oil is ideal to use for stir-frying because it has a high smoke point. Its high monounsaturated fat content makes it a healthy option, and it has a lovely mild nutty flavor.

vegan • gluten-free

Peanuts are rich in the antioxidant resveratrol, which has been linked to a reduced risk of cardiovascular disease. They're also a good source of niacin and folate. Brown rice contains a lot more fiber than refined white rice, so it helps to make you feel full for longer.

Brown rice salad with peanuts

Preparation time: 15 minutes
Cooking time: 25 minutes
Serves 4

1 cup brown rice

5½ oz snow peas, trimmed and thinly sliced

1 cup grape tomatoes, halved

½ cup unsalted roasted peanuts, coarsely chopped

4 scallions, trimmed and thinly sliced

2 tablespoons raisins

2 tablespoons coarsely chopped flat-leaf (Italian) parsley

2 tablespoons coarsely chopped mint

DRESSING

1½ tablespoons olive oil

1 tablespoon balsamic vinegar

1 tablespoon lemon juice

½ teaspoon granulated sugar

1 Cook the brown rice in a large saucepan of boiling water according to the package instructions or until just tender. Drain, transfer to a large bowl, and set aside.

2 Put the snow peas in a heatproof bowl. Pour over enough boiling water to cover, then set aside to blanch for 30 seconds. Refresh under cold running water. Drain and add to the rice. Add the tomatoes, peanuts, scallions, raisins, parsley, and mint.

3 To make the dressing, whisk the olive oil, balsamic vinegar, lemon juice, and sugar in a small bowl until the sugar has dissolved.

4 Drizzle the dressing over the salad and gently toss to combine, then serve.

tip This salad will keep in an airtight container in the refrigerator for up to 3 days. Bring to room temperature before serving.

Using spelt and lupin flour in the dough results in a more nutritious pasta than one made with regular wheat flour. Lupin flour is extremely rich in protein and fiber, and it lowers the GI of the pasta. Spelt flour is gentler on digestion than regular wheat flour, and can be tolerated by those with wheat intolerance. This pasta also works beautifully using just spelt flour.

Spelt and lupin pasta dough

Preparation time: 25 minutes
(plus 30 minutes resting)
Cooking time: 5 minutes
Serves 4–6

$3^{1}/_{3}$ cups spelt flour,
plus extra for dusting

1 cup lupin flour (or if unavailable, substitute with 1 cup spelt flour)

6 eggs

1 Put the spelt flour, lupin flour, and a pinch of sea salt in a food processor and pulse to combine. Add the eggs and process until the mixture forms large clumps.

2 Turn the dough out onto a clean work surface dusted lightly with spelt flour. Knead for 5 minutes, incorporating a little extra flour if the dough is too soft, until smooth and elastic. Wrap in plastic wrap and place in the refrigerator to rest for 30 minutes.

3 Divide the dough into four pieces and flatten each piece slightly. Pass one piece of dough through a pasta machine with the rollers set to the widest setting. Fold the pasta in half and turn 90 degrees. Repeat 3–4 times.

4 Reduce the setting by one notch and pass the dough through the rollers again. Continue reducing the setting and rolling the dough through once on each setting until you reach the second-thinnest setting. If the dough becomes too long to handle, cut the sheet into two pieces and roll each piece separately.

5 Cut the pasta sheets into the desired shapes. Lay the pasta flat on a tray, dust with a little flour, and set aside.

6 Repeat the rolling and cutting with the remaining pieces of pasta dough.

7 Cook the pasta in a large saucepan of lightly salted boiling water for 3–4 minutes or until al dente. Drain. Toss with your favorite sauce and serve.

Replacing some of the traditional wheat flour with lupin or besan flour increases the protein content and lowers the GI of these flat breads. Lupin and besan flour both have a strong, distinctive earthy smell, but it dissipates during cooking, so don't be put off by it.

Yogurt flat breads

Preparation time: 15 minutes
(plus 30 minutes resting)
Cooking time: 30 minutes
Makes 8

2 cups self-raising flour,
plus extra for dusting

1 cup lupin or besan flour

1 teaspoon baking powder

1 cup plain (natural) yogurt

1/2 teaspoon sea salt

1–2 tablespoons olive oil

1 Sift 1½ cups of the self-raising flour, the lupin or besan flour, and the baking powder together into a large bowl. Put the yogurt and salt in a separate large bowl and stir to combine. Using a wooden spoon, gradually stir in the flour mixture, then mix with your hands until a stiff dough forms.

2 Turn the dough out onto a lightly floured surface and knead for 5 minutes or until soft and smooth, gradually incorporating the remaining self-raising flour as the dough becomes sticky. Place in a lightly greased bowl, cover, and set aside to rest for 30 minutes.

3 Preheat the oven to 225°F. Divide dough into 8 pieces. Roll each piece out on a lightly floured surface to a circle approximately 6 inches in diameter.

4 Heat a large non-stick frying pan over medium–high heat and brush with some of the olive oil. Cook a flat bread for 2 minutes each side or until golden brown. Remove and transfer to the oven to keep warm. Repeat with the remaining oil and flat breads. Serve warm.

tip The dough should be quite soft and very pliable, but if it's too sticky, add a little more self-raising flour.

These flat breads are best eaten soon after they're made, while they're still warm.

« pictured page 154

gluten-free (see tips)

This version of an old favorite is made from whole foods such as walnuts, dates, coconut, and cacao, so it's healthier than regular peanut butter cups, as well as decadent. The trick is to eat only one.

Peanut butter cups

Preparation time: 25 minutes
Cooking time: 5 minutes
Makes 24

5½ oz dark chocolate, coarsely chopped
2 teaspoons coconut oil

BASE
½ cup walnut halves
¼ cup unsweetened dried coconut
2 tablespoons raw cacao or unsweetened cocoa powder
⅔ cup Medjool dates, pitted
2 teaspoons coconut oil

PEANUT FILLING
½ cup Medjool dates, pitted
¾ cup crunchy natural peanut butter
3 teaspoons honey

1 Line a 24-hole mini-muffin tin with paper cases.

2 To make the base, process the walnuts, coconut, and cacao in a food processor until finely chopped. With the motor running, add the dates a few at a time. Process until the mixture starts to come together. Add the coconut oil and process until well combined. Press a rounded teaspoon of mixture into the base of each paper case, smoothing the surface with the back of a spoon. Chill until firm.

3 To make the peanut filling, put the dates in a food processor and pulse until finely chopped. Add the peanut butter, honey, and a pinch of sea salt and process until smooth. Spoon a little peanut butter mixture into each paper case and smooth the surface. Freeze until firm.

4 Put the chocolate and coconut oil in a heatproof bowl over a saucepan of gently simmering water. Stir until melted and smooth. Spread a little chocolate mixture into each paper case and smooth the surface. Refrigerate until set. Serve chilled.

tips For a gluten-free version, use gluten-free chocolate.

Store the peanut butter cups in an airtight container in the refrigerator. They will keep for up to 2 weeks.

» **pictured pages 192–193**

Peanut butter cups

(see recipe page 191)

You can use lupin or besan flour in many baked goods by replacing 20–50% of the wheat flour with either lupin or besan flour. This not only significantly increases the protein and fiber content of the finished product, but also reduces the GI. People with a peanut allergy may also react to lupins.

Zucchini loaf

Preparation time: 15 minutes
Cooking time: 50 minutes
Serves 10–12

Oil spray, for greasing

¾ cup spelt flour

¾ cup lupin or besan flour

2 teaspoons baking powder

1 teaspoon ground cinnamon

¼ teaspoon freshly grated nutmeg

2 large zucchini, grated

½ cup brown or granulated sugar

½ cup raisins, chopped

⅓ cup sweetened dried cranberries

½ cup pecan halves, roughly chopped

2 teaspoons finely grated lemon zest

2 eggs

½ cup macadamia oil, or other mildly flavored nut or seed oil such as sunflower or safflower oil

1 teaspoon pure vanilla extract

1 Preheat the oven to 350°F. Grease a 3½-inch x 8-inch loaf pan with oil spray and line the base with parchment paper, allowing the paper to hang over the two long sides to form handles.

2 Sift the spelt flour, lupin flour, baking powder, cinnamon, and nutmeg into a large bowl. Stir in the zucchini, sugar, raisins, cranberries, pecans, and lemon zest.

3 Whisk the eggs, oil, and vanilla together in a small bowl. Add to the dry ingredients and stir to combine. Spoon into the prepared pan and smooth the surface with the back of the spoon.

4 Bake for 45–50 minutes or until the loaf is golden and a skewer inserted into the center comes out clean. If it's browning too quickly, cover the top loosely with foil. Set aside to cool for 5 minutes. Remove from the pan and set aside on a wire rack to cool completely.

carob & mesquite

carob & mesquite

Carob and mesquite are unique culinary legumes, being derived from the pods of trees rather than ground plants. Until recently, mesquite was harvested only from the wild for local indigenous consumption.

carob

CAROB IS NATIVE to the eastern Mediterranean, where it has been cultivated for at least 4000 years. It is a slow-growing tree with long, leathery seed pods.

The seeds, pulp, and pods of carob trees are all utilized. The seeds form the basis of locust bean gum, which is used in the food industry as a stabilizer and thickening agent, the pulp is used as animal feed, and the nutritious dark brown pods are roasted, dried, and milled to form carob powder.

Carob powder has its own distinctive taste, although it is similar in some ways to cocoa, and it can be used in cooking as a cocoa substitute.

Carob powder has some nutritional and other advantages, however, over cocoa. It has a higher protein content (8%) and does not contain caffeine, theobromine, or tyramine, all of which are found in cocoa and may have unwanted side effects, such as triggering headaches and migraines in some people. Carob is also free of oxalic acid, which can interfere with calcium absorption.

Carob is naturally gluten-free, contains less fat than cocoa, and is slightly sweeter than unsweetened cocoa powder. For this reason, when using carob powder as a substitute for cocoa, you can reduce the amount of sugar you use by 25–30%.

NUTRITION	PER 100 G (3½ OZ) CAROB POWDER	PER 100 G (3½ OZ) CAROB CHIPS
Energy	288 cal	512 cal
Protein	4.6 g	11.2 g
Fat	0.6 g	33.1 g
Saturated fat	0.1 g	31 g
Carbohydrate	49.1 g	44.4 g
Dietary fiber	39.8 g	3.3 g
Calcium	348 mg	370 mg
Potassium	827 mg	850 mg
Magnesium	0 mg	0 mg

mesquite

MESQUITE POWDER comes from the seed pods of the mesquite tree, which grows in the southwest United States and parts of South America. The indigenous peoples of these areas have traditionally eaten it as a staple food, grinding the seeds into powder and using it as a sweetener, a flour, and a beverage.

Mesquite powder is now emerging in modern cooking, finding its way onto the shelves of health food stores. It has a unique flavor and aroma and is extremely versatile, used in cooking as a spice or as a sweet flour. It has a spicy, nutty taste with delicious cinnamon, caramel, and even toasted coconut tones.

Mesquite can be used to replace some of the regular flour in baked goods such as breads, pancakes, muffins, cakes, and cookies. As a general rule, try substituting 2–3 tablespoons out of every cup of flour in a recipe with mesquite powder. Its higher sugar content means you need to use less sugar, and you may need to bake at a slightly lower temperature to prevent the sugars from burning.

Mesquite powder can be used as a natural sweetener, and its caramel-like flavor makes it a perfect fit for desserts, marrying well with flavors such as chocolate, coffee, dried fruit, and nuts. Try adding a spoonful of mesquite powder to smoothies and milkshakes for a rich, sweet taste.

Nutritionally speaking, mesquite, like all legumes, is packed with dietary fiber (about 28%) and is a good source of protein. It is rich in several minerals including calcium, magnesium, potassium, and zinc. It is also gluten-free and has a low GI of just 25.

NUTRITION	PER 100 G (3½ OZ) MESQUITE POWDER*
Energy	379 cal
Protein	16 g
Fat	3.4 g
Saturated fat	0 g
Carbohydrate	80 g
Dietary fiber	36 g
Calcium	520 mg
Potassium	0 mg
Magnesium	140 mg

* Accredited nutritional analysis for mesquite powder is unavailable because of mesquite's small production and relatively recent availability.

Coconut milk makes a great creamy smoothie. For a version that's lighter in taste and calories, try coconut water as a refreshing alternative.

Blueberry, coconut, and mesquite smoothies

Preparation time: 5 minutes
Cooking time: Nil
Serves 2

1⅓ cups (10½ fl oz) chilled coconut milk or coconut water

1 cup frozen blueberries

1 firm ripe banana, peeled and chopped

2 teaspoons mesquite powder (see tip)

2 teaspoons chia seeds

1 Put all the ingredients in a blender and blend until smooth and creamy. Divide between 2 serving glasses. Serve immediately.

tip Mesquite powder has a caramel, cinnamon, and coffee flavor that is delicious combined with blueberries and coconut. It's gluten-free and has a low GI, and it gives a naturally rich taste to a smoothie.

» **pictured page 202**

Macadamia oil is wonderful to use in baked goods. It has a delicious mild nutty taste that works beautifully in these muffins, and it is the richest natural source of monounsaturated fats (81%). Carob chips, unlike chocolate, do not contain caffeine.

Carob raspberry muffins

Preparation time: 10 minutes
Cooking time: 20 minutes
Makes 12

2 cups white spelt flour

1 tablespoon baking powder

1 teaspoon ground cinnamon

1 cup fresh or frozen raspberries (see tips)

½ cup demerara sugar

1 cup buttermilk

2 eggs

7 tablespoons macadamia oil, or other mildly flavored nut or seed oil such as sunflower or safflower oil

1 teaspoon pure vanilla extract

⅔ cup carob chips, coarsely chopped

1 Preheat the oven to 350°F. Line a 12-hole standard muffin tin with paper cases.

2 Sift the flour, baking powder, and cinnamon into a large bowl. Add the raspberries and sugar and stir to combine.

3 Whisk together the buttermilk, eggs, oil, and vanilla extract. Add to the dry ingredients and stir until just combined. Stir in the carob.

4 Divide the mixture between the prepared paper cases. Bake for 20–22 minutes or until golden. Transfer to a wire rack and set aside to cool.

tips You can replace the raspberries with fresh or frozen blueberries or cherries. Stirring the raspberries into the dry ingredients, rather than adding them last, prevents them from sinking during baking.

Muffins are best eaten on the day they are made, but they do freeze well. Wrap them individually in plastic wrap before freezing in an airtight container.

» **pictured pages 202–203**

Blueberry, coconut, and mesquite smoothies

(see recipe page 200)

Carob raspberry muffins

(see recipe page 201)

These truffles have a delicious silky texture and you won't believe they're not made from chocolate.

Carob, pistachio, and date truffles

Preparation time: 15 minutes
Cooking time: Nil
Makes 30

2 tablespoons carob powder (see tips)
½ cup shelled raw pistachios
2 tablespoons almond or cashew butter
1½ cups Medjool dates, pitted

1 Process the carob powder and ¼ cup of the pistachios in a food processor until the nuts are finely chopped.

2 Add the nut butter and pulse to combine. With the motor running, add the dates a few at a time. Process until all the dates are added and the mixture comes together, adding 1 teaspoon cold water if necessary. The mixture should be soft and pliable. Remove it from the food processor and bring it together completely with your hands. Set aside.

3 Process the remaining pistachios in a clean food processor until finely chopped, then transfer to a large plate. Roll heaped teaspoons of the date mixture into balls. Roll the truffles in the pistachios to lightly coat, shaking off any excess. Place in an airtight container and refrigerate.

tips You can replace the carob powder with unsweetened cocoa powder or raw cacao powder.

These truffles will keep in an airtight container in the refrigerator for up to 2 weeks. Remove them from the refrigerator 10 minutes before serving.

» **pictured pages 206–207**

Rolled oats are made from whole grains, and they're packed with beta glucan dietary fiber. Processing the oats gives these cookies a delicious texture. To make a dairy-free version, replace the butter with a dairy-free spread, and use soy carob chips.

Peanut carob chip cookies

Preparation time: 20 minutes
Cooking time: 15 minutes
Makes 30

1 cup rolled oats

2/3 cup firmly packed brown sugar

1/3 cup unsalted butter, softened

1/4 cup crunchy natural peanut butter

1 egg, lightly beaten

1 teaspoon pure vanilla extract

1 cup all-purpose flour

1/2 teaspoon baking powder

1/2 cup unsalted raw peanuts, coarsely chopped

1/3 cup small carob chips, coarsely chopped, plus 30 extra chips to decorate

1 Preheat the oven to 350°F. Line a large baking tray with parchment paper. Place the oats in a food processor and pulse until chopped, leaving some texture. Set aside.

2 Use an electric mixer to beat the sugar, butter, and peanut butter in a large bowl until pale and creamy. Add the egg and vanilla and beat until smooth. Sift the flour and baking powder over the butter mixture and stir until combined. Add the oats, peanuts, and chopped carob and stir to combine.

3 Roll tablespoons of the mixture into balls and place on the prepared tray. Flatten slightly and press a carob chip into the center of each. Bake for 12 minutes or until golden.

4 Cool on the tray for 5 minutes, then transfer to a wire rack to cool completely.

tip The cookies will keep in an airtight container for up to 1 week.

» **pictured page 207**

Carob, pistachio, and date truffles

(see recipe page 204)

**Peanut carob
chip cookies**

(see recipe page 205)

dairy-free • gluten-free

Mesquite is a delicious addition to spice rubs for grilled or barbecued meats, adding a touch of sweetness to balance the spice of the chili and pepper.

Grilled steak with mesquite rub

Preparation time: 10 minutes
Cooking time: 5 minutes
Serves 4

4 x 5½ oz sirloin steaks, fat trimmed
2 teaspoons coriander seeds
1 teaspoon black peppercorns
½ teaspoon dried chili flakes
½ teaspoon sea salt
1½ teaspoons mesquite powder
1 tablespoon olive oil
Baby arugula leaves, to serve
Freshly shaved parmesan cheese, to serve
Balsamic vinegar, to drizzle

1 Bring the steaks to room temperature. Combine the coriander seeds, peppercorns, chili flakes, and salt in a mortar and pestle. Pound until finely ground, then stir in the mesquite powder.

2 Rub the steaks evenly with the spice mixture, then drizzle with the olive oil. Preheat a grill pan or barbecue plate over high heat. Add the steaks and cook for 2–3 minutes each side or until cooked to your liking. Remove from the pan, cover loosely with foil, and set aside to rest for 2–3 minutes. Thickly slice.

3 Serve the steaks with arugula and parmesan, drizzled with balsamic vinegar.

tip You can use a spice grinder instead of a mortar and pestle to grind the spices.

» **pictured page 211**

Mesquite adds a delicious twist to these fruit buns. Its caramel–coffee-like aroma works beautifully with nuts such as walnuts, and with dried fruit. Feel free to use any type of fruit you like – sweetened dried cranberries and dried cherries work well.

Fruit, mesquite, and walnut buns

Preparation time: 30 minutes
(plus 1 hour 20 minutes proofing)
Cooking time: 20 minutes
Makes 10

1 cup lukewarm milk

**1½ cups all-purpose flour,
plus extra for dusting**

2 teaspoons dried yeast

2¼ tablespoons granulated sugar

½ cup whole-wheat flour

**2 tablespoons unsalted butter, diced,
plus extra for greasing**

**½ cup mixed dried fruit,
coarsely chopped**

½ cup walnut halves, coarsely chopped

1½ tablespoons mesquite powder

**1 teaspoon mixed spice
(pumpkin pie spice)**

Warmed apricot jam (jelly), to glaze

1 Put the milk, 2 tablespoons of the all-purpose flour, the yeast, and 1 teaspoon of the sugar in a medium bowl and whisk to combine. Set aside in a warm place for 10 minutes or until frothy.

2 Meanwhile, combine the remaining all-purpose flour and the whole-wheat flour in a large bowl. Rub the butter in with your fingertips until the mixture resembles breadcrumbs. Add the remaining sugar and the dried fruit, walnuts, mesquite powder, spice, and a pinch of sea salt and stir to combine.

3 Add the milk mixture and stir with a wooden spoon until the mixture comes together to form a sticky dough. Turn onto a lightly floured surface and knead for 5–6 minutes or until smooth and elastic. Place in a lightly greased bowl, cover, and set aside in a warm place for 1 hour or until doubled in size.

4 Preheat the oven to 350°F. Line a large baking tray with parchment paper. Punch the dough down with your fist, turn onto a lightly floured surface, and knead lightly for 1–2 minutes or until smooth. Divide the dough into 10 pieces. Roll each piece into a ball, then flatten slightly to form a bun shape. Place on the prepared tray, cover, and set aside in a warm place to rest for 20 minutes.

5 Bake for 20 minutes or until the buns are golden. Remove them from the oven and brush the tops with warmed jam to glaze. Serve warm.

tips The buns are best eaten warm, or on the day they are made. They can also be frozen. Wrap them individually in plastic wrap before freezing in an airtight container.

**Grilled steak with
mesquite rub**

(see recipe page 208)

**Freekeh and bean salad
with almonds and raisins**

(see recipe page 73)

These biscotti make the perfect treat to have with a cup of tea. The mesquite lends a natural sweetness, and delicious coffee/caramel flavor that is a perfect match with the chocolate and cranberries.

Mesquite, cranberry, and chocolate biscotti

Preparation time: 20 minutes
Cooking time: 45 minutes
Makes about 40

²/₃ **cup granulated sugar**

2 eggs

2 cups all-purpose flour, plus extra for dusting

1¹/₂ **tablespoons mesquite powder**

¹/₃ **cup raw almonds**

¹/₃ **cup sweetened dried cranberries**

¹/₄ **cup white or dark chocolate chips**

1 Preheat the oven to 350°F. Line a large baking tray with parchment paper.

2 Use an electric mixer with a whisk attachment to whisk the sugar and eggs for 3 minutes or until they have increased in volume and are thick and pale.

3 Sift in the flour and mesquite powder and stir with a wooden spoon until almost combined. Add the almonds, cranberries, and chocolate chips and mix with your hands until well combined.

4 Dust your hands with extra flour. Divide the mixture in half and shape into 2 logs about 6 inches long. Place the logs on the prepared tray and flatten slightly to ¾ inch thick. Bake for 20 minutes or until firm. Remove from the oven and cool completely on the tray.

5 Reduce the oven temperature to 225°F. Cut the logs into slices about ³/₈ inch thick. Place in a single layer on oven trays and bake, turning once, for 25–30 minutes or until the biscotti are completely dry. Transfer to a wire rack and set aside to cool.

tip Biscotti will keep in an airtight container for up to 1 month.

dairy-free • gluten-free

Mesquite powder adds a natural sweetness and richness to this mousse. The avocado makes it creamy (without any cream!), and the cocoa powder gives an intense chocolate flavor.

Raw chocolate and mesquite mousse

Preparation time: 10 minutes
Cooking time: Nil
Serves 4

2 ripe avocados, stone removed, peeled (see tips)

1/4 cup honey

1/4 cup unsweetened cocoa or raw cacao powder, sifted

2 tablespoons mesquite powder, plus extra to garnish

1/3 cup coconut cream

1 Process the avocado, honey, cocoa, and mesquite in a food processor until smooth. Add the coconut cream and process until smooth and creamy, adding a little extra coconut cream if the mousse is too thick.

2 Spoon the mousse into 4 serving dishes. Cover and refrigerate until chilled. Garnish with a little extra mesquite powder and serve.

tips For a smooth and luscious texture, it's essential to use ripe avocados in this recipe.

For a vegan version, you can replace the honey with rice malt syrup. You may need to add a few extra teaspoons because it is not as sweet as honey.

» **pictured pages 214–215**

**Mesquite, cranberry,
and chocolate biscotti**

(see recipe page 212)

**Raw chocolate and
mesquite mousse**

(see recipe page 213)

Mesquite powder is extracted from the seed pods of the mesquite tree, a leguminous shrubby tree found in the southwest of the United States and in parts of South America. It can be used as a natural sweetener, meaning you need to add less sugar, and it lends a caramel–coffee flavor to these delicious puddings.

Coffee and fig self-saucing puddings

Preparation time: 20 minutes
(plus 10 minutes soaking)
Cooking time: 25 minutes
Serves 6

½ cup finely chopped dried figs
1 cup self-raising flour
2 tablespoons mesquite powder
¼ cup firmly packed brown sugar
⅔ cup milk
1 egg
4½ tablespoons unsalted butter, melted and cooled, plus extra for greasing
Fresh raspberries, to serve

SAUCE
⅓ cup firmly packed brown sugar
1 tablespoon mesquite powder
¼ cup strong espresso coffee

1 Preheat the oven to 350°F. Grease six 5 fl oz ovenproof dishes and place on a large baking tray. Put the figs in a heatproof bowl, add ⅓ cup boiling water and leave to soak for 10 minutes. Drain and set aside.

2 Sift the flour and mesquite into a medium bowl. Stir in the brown sugar. Whisk the milk, egg, and butter together in a large bowl. Add to the flour mixture and stir until just combined, then stir in the soaked figs. Pour the mixture into the prepared ovenproof dishes and smooth the surface with the back of a spoon.

3 To make the sauce, combine the sugar and mesquite in a small bowl. Sprinkle evenly over the pudding mixture. Combine the espresso and 1 cup boiling water in a small heatproof bowl. Carefully pour the espresso mixture over the sugar mixture.

4 Bake for 20–25 minutes or until a cake-like topping has formed and a skewer inserted into the center of a pudding comes out clean. Stand for 5 minutes, then serve with raspberries.

acknowledgments

I would like to thank the team at Murdoch Books, and in particular Corinne Roberts, for believing in my dream of shooting a book in the beautiful Byron Bay hinterland, and making it a reality. To Susanne Geppert and Madeleine Kane for designing such beautiful pages, Virginia Birch for keeping me on schedule, and Kerryn Burgess for her meticulous editing. Thanks also to the Grains & Legumes Nutrition Council for assistance with research.

A big thank you to Julie Renouf for her stunning photography — you are a magician with natural light — and to Kristine Duran-Thiessen for sourcing such beautiful ceramics and then for making the food come to life on the plate. You are both incredibly talented, wonderful friends, and such a pleasure to work with. A very big thank you also to Anton and Kristine for opening your house and letting us shoot in one of the most beautiful places in the world, the magical macadamia farm "Agnutta."

To my family — thank you Pete, Row, Max, and Darby for taste-testing almost every dish in the book, and my little girl Harriet (aka the midge) for putting up with a mother who sometimes works too hard (you constantly remind me of the things that actually matter in life). And finally and most importantly, I would like to thank my parents, Robert and Jean Freer. Without your continuous love and support, this book simply could not have happened.

index

Appetite by Random House® edition published 2016

Text copyright © 2015 Chrissy Freer
Design copyright © 2015 Murdoch Books
Photography copyright © 2015 Julie Renouf

Originally published in a slightly different form in Australia
by Murdoch Books, an imprint of Allen & Unwin, Australia.

All rights reserved. The use of any part of this publication, reproduced,
transmitted in any form or by any means electronic, mechanical,
photocopying, recording, or otherwise, or stored in a retrieval system
without the prior written consent of the publisher—or in the case of
photocopying or other reprographic copying, license from the Canadian
Copyright Licensing Agency—is an infringement of the copyright law.

Appetite by Random House® and colophon are registered trademarks
of Penguin Random House LLC.

Library and Archives of Canada Cataloguing in Publication is available
upon request.

ISBN: 978−0−147−53012−7
eBook ISBN: 978−0−147−53013−4

Printed and bound in China

OVEN GUIDE: You may find cooking times vary depending on the oven
you are using. For convection ovens, as a general rule, set the oven
temperature to 35°F (20°C) lower than indicated in the recipe.

MEASURES GUIDE: We have used 20 ml (4 teaspoon) tablespoon
measures. If you are using a 15 ml (3 teaspoon) tablespoon, add
an extra teaspoon of the ingredient for each tablespoon specified.

The author, publisher, and stylist would like to thank the following
ceramicists for lending their works for use in the production of this book:
Marie-Helene Clauzon, Anna-Karina Elias, Robert Gordon Australia,
Samantha Robinson, and Susan Simonini. Thanks also to Fruitos in Byron
Bay and Daley's Gourmet Meats in Ballina for providing beautiful produce.

Published in Canada by Appetite by Random House®, a division of
Penguin Random House Canada Limited

www.penguinrandomhouse.ca

10 9 8 7 6 5 4 3 2 1

appetite
by RANDOM HOUSE

Penguin
Random
House